The
Barefoot
Woman

Selected works by Scholastique Mukasonga

Our Lady of the Nile
Cockroaches
Igifu

The Barefoot Woman

Scholastique Mukasonga

Translated by Jordan Stump

This edition first published in the
United Kingdom in 2022 by
Daunt Books Originals
83 Marylebone High Street
London W1U 4QW

1

A CIP catalogue record for this title
is available from the British Library.

ISBN 978-1-914198-08-3

Typeset by Marsha Swan

Printed and bound by TJ Books Ltd

www.dauntbookspublishing.co.uk

The
Barefoot
Woman

Often, in the middle of one of those never-ending chores that fill a woman's day (sweeping the yard, shelling and sorting beans, weeding the sorghum patch, tilling the soil, digging sweet potatoes, peeling and cooking bananas . . .), my mother would pause and call out to us, her three youngest daughters, not by our baptismal names, Jeanne, Julienne, Scholastique, but by our real names, the ones given us at birth by our father, names whose meaning, always open to interpretation, seemed to sketch out our future lives: 'Umubyeyi, Uwamubyirura, Mukasonga!' Mama would give us a lingering stare, as if she were going away for a long time, as if – she who rarely left the enclosure, who never strayed too far from her field, except on Sundays, for Mass – she were making ready for a great voyage, as if she would never again see the three of us gathered around her. And in a voice that didn't sound like hers, that seemed like something from another world, a voice that filled us with terror, she would say: 'When I die, when you see me lying dead before you, you'll have to cover my body. No one must see me. A mother's dead body is not to be seen. You'll have to cover me, my daughters, that's your job and no one else's. No one must see a mother's corpse. Otherwise it will follow you, it will chase you . . . it will haunt you until it's your turn to die, when you too will need someone to cover your body.'

Those words frightened us. We didn't understand them – even today I'm not sure I understand them – but they sent a chill down our spines. We were convinced we had to keep one eye on Mama at every moment, that we had to be ready, should death suddenly take her, to cover her with her *pagne* so no one could glimpse her lifeless body. And it's true that death hovered insistently over every deportee in Nyamata, but to three little girls it seemed to threaten our mother most of all, like a silent leopard stalking its prey. All day long, our anxious thoughts stayed close by her side. Mama was always the first one up in the morning, long before the rest of us were awake, to go off for her daily walk around the village. We trembled as we waited for her to come back, relieved when we finally glimpsed her through the coffee plants, washing her feet in the dewy grass. When two of us went to fetch water or wood, we always told the third: 'Whatever you do, keep an eye on Mama.' And our hearts knew no peace until we came home and saw her shelling beans under the big manioc. But schooldays were the worst, when my mind filled with horrific pictures that blotted out the teacher's lesson, pictures of Mama's corpse lying in front of the termite mound she so loved to sit on.

I never did cover my mother's body with her *pagne*. No one was there to cover her. Maybe the murderers lingered over the corpse their machetes had dismembered. Maybe blood-drunk hyenas and dogs fed on her flesh. Her poor remains dissolved into the stench of the genocide's monstrous mass grave, and maybe now, but this too I don't know, maybe now she's deep in the jumble of some ossuary, bones among bones, one skull among others.

Mama, I wasn't there to cover your body, and all I have left is words – words in a language you didn't understand – to do as you asked. And I'm all alone with my feeble words, and on the pages of my notebook, over and over, my sentences weave a shroud for your missing body.

SAVING THE CHILDREN

Maybe the Hutu authorities put in charge of the newly independent Rwanda by the Belgians and the Church were hoping the Tutsis of Nyamata would gradually be wiped out by sleeping sickness and famine. In any case, the region they chose to send them to, the Bugesera, seemed inhospitable enough to make those internal exiles' survival more than unlikely. And yet they survived, for the most part. Their courage and solidarity let them face the hostile wilderness, farm a first little patch of land that didn't completely spare them from hunger but at least kept them alive. And little by little the displaced families' makeshift huts became villages – Gitwe, Gitagata, Cyohoha – where people struggled to recapture some semblance of everyday life, which of course did little to soften the crushing sorrow of exile.

But the Tutsis of Nyamata weren't slow to realise that the tenuous survival they seemed to have been granted was only a temporary reprieve. The soldiers of the Gako Camp, built between the villages and the nearby border with Burundi, were there to remind them that they were no longer exactly human beings but *inyenzi*, cockroaches, insects it was only right to persecute and eventually exterminate.

I can still picture the soldiers from Gako bursting into our house, a rifle butt crumpling the piece of sheet metal we used as a door. They claimed they were looking for a photo of King Kigeri or covert letters from exiles in Burundi or Uganda. All that, of course, was pure pretext. Long before, the displaced families of Nyamata had thrown out everything that might possibly incriminate them.

I don't know how many times the soldiers came to pillage our houses and terrorise the people inside. My memory has compressed all those acts of violence into one single scene. It's like a film playing over and over. The same images again and again, engraved in my mind by my little-girl fear, later to return in my nightmares.

The scene that unfolds before my memory is peaceful at first. The entire family is gathered in our one room, around the three stones of the hearth. It must be July or August, the dry season, summer holidays, because André and Alexia are there too, back from their school a long way from Nyamata. Night has fallen, but the moon isn't full, because we aren't sitting outside behind the house, enjoying its light. Everything seems strangely calm, as if the soldiers are yet to pay us their first sudden, brutal visit. Evidently Mama has taken none of the extraordinary precautions I'll talk about soon. I see everyone in their usual places. My mother Stefania is squatting on her mat against the outer wall. Alexia is close by the fire, maybe trying to read one of her schoolbooks by the flickering light of the flames, maybe only pretending. I can't make out my father in the dimness at the far end of the room; I can only hear the continual, monotonous clicks of the rosary he never stops fingering. Julienne, Jeanne, and I are pressed close together near the front door that opens onto the dirt road. Mama has just set down the family plate of sweet potatoes in front of us, but we haven't yet begun to eat. We hang on André's every word as he sits in our one chair at the little table built specially for him – the boy, the student, the hope of the family – by our older brother Antoine. André is telling stories from school, and for us they're like news from a distant world, an amazing, inaccessible world, and they make us laugh, laugh, laugh . . .

And then, all of a sudden, the clang of the sheet metal crashing down: I just have time to snatch up my little sister and roll with her off to one side, dodging the boot that grazes her face, the boot that tramples the sweet potatoes and buckles the metal plate like cardboard. I make myself as small as I can, I wish I could burrow into the ground, I hide Jeanne beneath a fold of my *pagne*, I stifle her sobs, and when I dare to look up again, I see three soldiers overturning our baskets and jugs, throwing the mats we'd hung from the ceiling out into the yard.

One of them has grabbed hold of André, and now he's dragging him toward the door (I think I can see my brother's struggling body go past, slowly, slowly, just beside my face) and my father races forward as if he could hold back the soldier, and I hear my mother and Alexia crying out. I squeeze my eyes shut as hard as I can so I won't have to see. Everything goes dark, I want to burrow deep underground . . .

The silence makes me open my eyes again. My father is helping a wincing André to his feet. My mother and Alexia are cleaning up the spilled beans. Now, from next door, comes the same sound of boots, the same shrieks, the same sobs, the same crash of breaking jugs . . .

My mother had only one thought in her head, one single project day in and day out, one sole reason to go on surviving: saving her children. For that she tried every possible tactic, devised every conceivable stratagem. We needed some way to flee, we needed someplace to hide.

The best thing, obviously, was to take cover in the dense bramble thickets that bordered our field. But for that we'd need time. Mama was forever on guard, constantly listening for noises. Ever since the day when they burned our house in Magi, when she first heard that dull roar of hatred, like a monstrous beehive's hum racing toward us, I think she'd developed a sixth sense, the sense of an animal forever on the lookout for predators. She could make out the faintest, most faraway sound of boots on the road. 'Listen,' she would say, 'they're back.' We listened intently. We heard only the familiar sounds of the neighbours, the usual rustles of the savannah. 'They're back,' my mother said again. 'Quick, run and hide.' Often she only had time to give us a sign. We scrambled under the bushes, and a moment later, peering out from our hiding place, we saw the patrol at the end of the road, and we trembled as we wondered if they'd break into our house, ravage and steal our meagre belongings, our few baskets of sorghum or beans, the few ears of corn we'd been foolish enough to put by.

But we had to be ready for anything: sometimes the soldiers were too quick even for my mother's sharp ear. And so, for those times when we wouldn't be able to reach the brush, she left armloads of wild grass in the middle of the field, mounds just big enough for her three little girls to slip into when the alarm was sounded. She kept a mental catalogue of what she thought would be the safest hiding places in the bush. She discovered the deep burrows dug by the anteaters. She was convinced we could slither into them, and so with Antoine's help she widened the tunnels and camouflaged the entrances under piles of grasses and branches. Jeanne made herself even tinier than she was to wriggle into the anteater's lair. Sometimes, despite all my mother's advice and encouragement, Jeanne couldn't quite make it. A little concerned, I asked Stefania what would happen when the anteater wanted to come home. I've forgotten her answer.

Mama left nothing to chance. Often, as night fell, she called a dress rehearsal. And so we knew exactly how to scurry into the brambles, how to dive under the dried grasses. Even in our panic at hearing the boots on the dirt road, we scurried straight for the thickets or burrows where Mama had taught us to lie low.

The displaced families' huts had only one door, which opened onto the road. To ease our escape, Mama cut a second way out, opening onto the field and the bush. But soon that back door, more or less concealed like the hiding places she'd made in the brambles, was of no use at all. Once (with helicopters to help them) they'd beaten back the ill-fated Inyenzi offensive launched from Burundi by Tutsi refugees, the soldiers of the Gako camp lost all fear of ambushes and attacks. No more did they keep to the dirt road they'd always carefully followed. Now their patrols tramped freely across country, all the way to the Burundi border. Now danger could just as well burst from the bush as come down the road; no more were our thorny hiding places the impregnable refuges my mother found so reassuring. And so she set about making hiding places inside the house itself. Against the mud walls she stacked big urns and baskets, almost as tall as grain bins, for Julienne and Jeanne to crawl behind if the soldiers burst in. I was already too big to squeeze into the shelter of the urns' black bellies or the baskets' elegant curves. My only recourse was to dive under my parents' bed. Those hiding places were meant more to comfort us than anything else, because they never fooled anyone, least of all the soldiers, who flushed us out in no time with vigorous kicks, all the while calling us cockroaches or little snakes.

Mama was never satisfied with her survival strategies. She was forever coming up with improvements to her camouflage, forever finding new refuges for her children. But deep down she knew there was only one sanctuary, only one way we could ensure our survival: crossing the border, leaving for Burundi, as so many Tutsis already had. But she never once thought of taking that way out herself. Neither my father nor my mother ever considered going into exile. I think they'd made up their minds to die in Rwanda. They would wait there to be killed, they would let themselves be murdered, but the children had to survive. And so my mother worked out every detail of our escape to Burundi, in case of emergency. She went off alone into the bush, scouting for trails that might lead to the border. She marked out a path, and under her guidance, not quite understanding why, we played that strange game of follow-the-leader.

Everything at home sat ready for the big departure, which might be announced at any moment, set off by rumours of massacres going around Nyamata, rifle shots in the night, the local governor's threats, a neighbour's arrest . . . A few sweet potatoes, some bananas, a little calabash of sorghum beer were always left wrapped up in a piece of *pagne*. We girls were meant to take that bundle along when we slipped away and set out for Burundi. It would accompany us into exile. My sisters and I refused to look at it, because to us it was a dark omen of the miseries awaiting us.

But it was Alexia and André that most worried my mother. They weren't there with the rest of us. They were at school, and wouldn't be back until the holidays. Mama imagined the worst: one day Alexia and André would come home and find no one there. The house would have been sacked and burned, she and Cosma would have been killed, and at least one of the three girls, or so she hoped, would have managed to escape from the killers and find her way to Burundi. But then what would become of Alexia and André? They'd have to find enough strength after their long walk from school to head straight for the border and face the many dangers they'd find on the way: patrols, elephants, buffalo . . . And so, in prearranged places, under a stone, near a stump, she buried provisions – beans, sweet potatoes. I helped her dig the holes, line them with fine grasses, make sure some air could get in. But of course we had to change the supplies regularly, and then we ate the slightly spoilt food buried by a mother's love.

You always had to be on your guard, so my mother took great pains to keep up with the goings-on in the area. Especially in Nyamata, home to the local government, the missionaries and their church, the marketplace. She interrogated anyone she saw coming back from Nyamata, trying to detect presages of a coming wave of arrests or murders. Had anyone heard tell of a meeting at the mayor's, had they seen a big car from Kigali in front of the town hall? Had anyone spotted army trucks crossing the iron bridge over the Nyabarongo? Were there huge crowds at the market, were there fistfights? What were people saying in the bars? And at Mass, in his sermon, did Father Canoni go on a little too long about loving your neighbour? And what was the teacher saying, the only one with a radio? Stefania carefully evaluated the information, decoded the rumours, divined the imminence or absence of a threat.

But you also had to stay abreast of the neighbours' doings. She suspected them of planning to flee to Burundi without telling her. 'One fine morning,' she sometimes sighed, 'we're going to wake up and find ourselves all alone. Everyone will have left for Burundi without a word to us.' Her suspicion was particularly focused on Pancrace, just next door, who she was sure was secretly making all sorts of plans to get out. 'That Pancrace,' she would say, 'he's a devious one, I know he's found some way of saving his family, but he won't tell a soul.' On the pretext of borrowing some fire (when in fact the first thing she did in the morning was to check that the coals were still glowing under the ash), or a little salt, or a handful of beans, she would hurry next door and discreetly look around for signs of an upcoming departure. Soon she decided that Pancrace was digging a tunnel out into the bush. With the help of Antoine, she set out to do the same, with the entrance under the big parental bed. At the end of the week, as soon he came back from his job as a gardener at the Agronomical Institute in Karama, not even giving him a moment to rest after his twenty-kilometre walk, she handed him the hoe. Crouched at the edge of the hole, she gave Antoine his instructions as he slowly disappeared into the depths. Fortunately for Antoine, Operation Tunnel soon proved unfeasible, and the work was promptly suspended. But Mama remained as sure as ever that wily Pancrace had come up with many other undisclosed plans to save his life and his family's.

My mother's watchfulness never waned. It grew doubly sharp in the evening, at dinnertime, since it was most often at nightfall, or sometimes at dawn, that the soldiers burst in to ransack the houses and terrorise their inhabitants. She had no intention of letting our shared plate of beans or bananas distract her, so Stefania never ate with us. Once we were served, she hurried to the far end of the field, at the edge of the savannah. For many long minutes she stared into the tangle of thorn trees, listening for the slightest unusual noise. If she spotted the camouflaged uniforms of the patrolling soldiers, she raced back to the house and told us, '*Twajwemo* – we're not alone.' With that we had to keep quiet, not move, be ready to bound into our hiding places, hoping we'd be spared for this evening at least.

If she found everything normal, she would gaze on us for a long while in silence. Nothing pleased her more than watching her children eat. She'd saved them from starvation, working for the Bageseras in exchange for a few sweet potatoes, carving farmland from the inhospitable bush by her tireless labour. Day after day she won out over the implacable destiny we'd been condemned to because we were Tutsis. Again today, her children were still alive at her side. She'd snatched them away from death's clutches. She looked at the three of us, Julienne, Jeanne, Scholastique. This evening we were alive. There might never be another evening.

'In Rwanda,' Mama used to say, 'women were proud to have children. Many children. Especially boys. But in Nyamata they tremble in terror when they give birth. Not for themselves, but for their children. Especially the boys. They know they'll be killed. They know that one day or another, soon or far in the future, they'll be killed. Look at Gaudenciana, across the way, she should be happy and proud. Every woman in the village should envy her. She has seven children. Seven sons. What more could a mother want? And still she looks at her sons with sadness and despair. She never lets them out of her sight. She wants them beside her at every moment. She wouldn't let them go to school. She doesn't even send them to fetch water. She's afraid they'll never come back from Lake Cyohoha. They've never been to the market in Nyamata. It's as if all they ever do is wait for death to come. And it's not just the boys. Women, girls, their turn will come. You know how they killed Merciana . . .'

Everyone in Nyamata had seen how they killed Merciana, everyone looked on as she was put to death, and the women understood that they wouldn't be spared either, no more than their children. It happened back when the exiles were still staying in that cramped little school in Nyamata. The families had built little huts in the school-yard to escape the closeness of the classrooms. Merciana belonged to an important family from Magi. They'd been deported to Nyamata like everyone else, but the father, whose life had been threatened, had managed to flee to Burundi. Merciana was the real head of her family, an 'evolved person', people said back then. I don't know where she went to school, but she could read and write. Knowing how to write is a dangerous thing when you have a father in Burundi. You're automatically suspected of corresponding with the Tutsis plotting their return to Rwanda, of being a spy, of passing information to people on this side of the border who might try to lend a hand. Not to mention that you might be hiding weapons. The mayor's thugs were always coming and questioning Merciana, searching her shabby little hut. We could hear the sobs of Merciana's brothers and sisters, her mother's pleas. And then one day they came with two soldiers. They grabbed Merciana. They dragged her out to the middle of the schoolyard, where everyone could see. They pulled her clothes off. They left her completely naked. The women shielded their children behind their *pagnes*. Slowly the two soldiers shouldered their rifles. 'They didn't aim for her heart,' Mama said again and again, 'they aimed for her breasts, only her breasts. They wanted to tell us Tutsi women, "Don't bear any children, because when you bring them into this world you're giving them death. You're not bearers of life any more, you're bearers of death."'

THE TEARS OF THE MOON

Needless to say, Stefania kept an eye out for omens, and there were many. There were signs in the sky: a halo around the moon, which turned from the beautiful light colour of *ikimuri* – cow's milk butter – to a dull red, like the dry-season dirt, blood-red spatters peppering the clouds. And then there were the waters of Lake Cyohoha suddenly becoming viscous and brown, like the river of Egypt under Moses's staff, according to Papa's Bible. And the crows: they flew up from the valley, from the big swamps where no one ever goes. Their black hordes turned circles over the village, and we plugged up our ears to silence their strident shrieks. There was no doubting it: they'd been sent by the *abazimu*, the spirits of the dead, and their sinister cries called out to us, 'Soon you'll be with us, adrift in the grey fog of the dead floating over the papyrus.'

There were more of those bad omens all the time. Old women with dried-out breasts suddenly had milk, babies refused to leave their mothers' bellies. Fortunately, there was sometimes a way to ward off a cruel fate. Stefania knew all the plants that brought good fortune, and all the proper places to leave them inside the house. She also dipped them in water and generously sprinkled the perimeter of the yard and the field. Only rainwater would do for that ritual purification. The fetid water from Lake Cyohoha was considered pernicious, it was the brew of sorrow. We always boiled it before we drank it, not for hygienic reasons, but simply to drive out or at least weaken the malevolent essence it held. Papa preferred methods more acceptable to Catholic orthodoxy. Next to Mama's plants he laid fronds, like palm leaves, blessed on Palm Sunday by the Fathers. If he suspected that the virtues of the holy water had slightly evaporated, he reinvigorated the desiccated leaves with a drop of Lourdes water from a tiny vial that, as leader of the Legion of Mary, he'd got from the missionaries along with his glasses.

But the most terrifying of all these presages were the tears that flowed from the moon.

There were three special plants in the yard at our house in Gitagata, special in their size and the use we made of them. A coffee plant had mysteriously sprouted on the flat termite mound my mother used as a bench. Fertilised by our kitchen scraps and the beans' cooking water, it had grown very tall, and now it served as a parasol. Also for shade, we'd planted a tall manioc at the end of the yard: we sheltered under its leaves to rest after we'd threshed the sorghum or beans. Antoine had brought the rootstock home from Karama, and its gigantic leaves were nothing like the manioc we farmed in our fields (fighting back our misgivings about the poisonous roots of that plant forced on us by the Belgians).

In the middle of the banana grove, towering over the thick mass of the leaves, stood a third plant, this one charged with mystery: a castor plant, very tall, very graceful. We didn't know where the seed had come from, and how it could have taken root in the banana grove's dark shade. We wondered how its long, slender stalk could have pierced through the thick green veil, how it had managed to raise such slender branches so high into the sky, so high, it seemed to us, that they must touch the moon. My little sisters and I clamoured to eat the seeds. 'Roast us some of those!' we said to Mama. Our parents refused. That wasn't 'respectable' food, they thought. Ngoboka, the pagan, had secretly given us a taste of that forbidden fruit. Julienne and I immediately concluded that we'd found a substitute, almost every bit as tasty, for the peanuts we grew but weren't allowed to eat: the whole peanut harvest was sold at the market to buy salt and the blue fabric Stefania used for our school uniforms. We thought they owed us those delicious seeds. Finally Mama gave in to our endless pleas. 'Water purifies everything,' she said again and again, like an incantation, as she gave the seeds a long soak in rainwater, then dried them, roasted them, and to our great delight presented us each with a handful of that coveted treat.

Longingly as we looked at the castor plant, it terrified us too. It was on its leaves that the tears of the moon fell. Those tears were the colour and consistency of slightly soft butter, Stefania said, and they slid over the leaves, then flowed in oily drips down the plant and collected in pale puddles at its base. This happened only when the moon was full.

I never did see those tears of the moon, and neither did my sisters. And Stefania had no intention of showing us, because she said that butter from the sky had nothing in common with the life-giving manna that fed the Israelites in Papa's Bible. No, it was a grim omen that foretold the most horrible sorrows for the family. 'The moon wept again,' she would announce when we got up. Long before dawn, she'd hurried out to the fateful tree. That lunar butter couldn't be given a chance to melt in the first rays of the sun. 'Otherwise,' she claimed, 'it would spread everywhere!' The tears of the moon had to be buried in a snake hole as quickly as possible, like the teeth of illegitimate children.

Such children are never rejected, of course, they're brought up just like the others, but they're dangerous, all the same – they might bring unhappiness to a family – and that danger is at its peak when they lose their baby teeth. You have to carefully take up each tooth and bury it quick as you can in a snake hole. And so, like those teeth, the tears of the moon vanished into the reptile's lair, as if swallowed by the very entrails of the earth.

The tears of the moon set off a terrible panic in our house. We thought the soldiers were surely coming for us, and maybe this time it would end badly, they'd take away Papa, Antoine, and André if they were home. And then Papa and my brothers would never come back, just like the shopkeepers and teachers they'd arrested in 1963, never to be seen again. And maybe a soldier would start shooting, you never know why a soldier starts shooting . . . Mama inspected the hiding places, and again made us practise the survival tactics she'd taught us. The tension grew as the day went by. My parents called us to dinner long before sundown. They barricaded the house, knowing perfectly well it would do little to protect us. My parents and Antoine stayed up all night. They took turns keeping watch. Every now and then they went out to look down the road, to peer into the bush, never relaxing their vigilance, ready to give us the signal to run. And often, as I recall, the moon had wept for good reason.

STEFANIA'S HOUSE

The displaced people's shacks were lined up along the dirt road, behind a row of coffee plants. We called them Tripolo houses. Needless to say, Tripolo is a white person's name. I never knew who this Tripolo was, or if his name really was Tripolo. He could have been an administrator in Nyamata or an agronomist, but one thing is certain: he was Belgian. No refugee had ever seen this Tripolo, of course, but his name made a good bogeyman. If a child was caught being naughty, his mother would tell him: 'Tripolo's going to come get you!' Closing my eyes, I pictured Tripolo with a fat belly sticking out over his khaki shorts, his socks up to his knees, sweating under his pith helmet as he chased after children, brandishing his whip – his *ikiboko*. In any case people said it was Tripolo who ordered that stakes be driven into the ground to hold up the cheap sheet metal the refugees were supposed to use as walls for their houses.

To Mama, that Tripolo house was not a house at all. The mud walls that Papa and Antoine had put up between the poles were too straight, too square, the corners they made were too hard, the edges too sharp, it seemed Stefania was forever colliding with them, scraping herself on them, like a trapped, frantic insect. Disoriented, she searched in vain for a friendly curve to nestle into, the kind she remembered, a curve that cradled her back just so. She cursed the rectangular door that let the brazen sunlight come pouring in. 'We live outside,' she never stopped saying. 'We can't even eat without strangers walking past and looking straight into our mouths!' For her, as for all Rwandans, that was the height of obscenity. And those young coffee plants certainly wouldn't protect us from the indiscreet or spiteful stares that neighbours or passers-by could be counted on to give her and her children. A Tripolo house was open to every curse, every mortal threat that hung over the family. Mama felt exposed to shame and sorrow, defenceless, without even the last resort of exile.

For a long time the refugees hoped they would soon be going home, back 'to Rwanda', as they said. But they lost all such illusions after the bloody reprisals of early 1963. Now they understood – and the soldiers from Gako were there to remind them, if they needed reminding – that they'd never cross the Nyabarongo again, never again see the hills they'd been driven from. They were doomed to languish forever, they and their children, in the place of exile and disgrace that the Bugesera had always been, since Rwanda's earliest days. A land that our stories called the very end of the inhabited world, a place of banishment, so said our traditions, for treasonous warriors, dishonoured daughters, and adulterous wives, a place for them to be lost forever, powerless to find their way back to Rwanda. At the edge of the swamps, where the spirits of the dead wandered without end, and where, for many of us, death was indeed waiting.

Not long after we were moved to Gitagata, Stefania decided it was time to build an *inzu* behind the Tripolo house. An *inzu*: the kind of house that was as vital to her as water to a fish, as oxygen to a human being. Not because she'd come to accept her fate as an exile – she never resigned herself to that – but because she knew it was only in the ancestral dwelling place that she'd find the strength and courage she'd need to face our misfortunes, to replenish the energy she unstintingly expended to save her children from a death that an incomprehensible fate had planned out for them.

Stefania's house, the house where she could live the life of a real wife, a real mother, was a house made of straw woven like a basket, it was an *inzu* (and I'll keep its name in Kinyarwanda, because the only words French gives me to describe it sound contemptuous: hut, shanty, shack ...). There are precious few houses like Stefania's left in Rwanda today. Now they're in museums, like the skeletons of huge beasts dead for millions of years. But in my memory the *inzu* is not that empty carcass, it's a house full of life, of children's laughter, of the young girls' lively chatter, the quiet singsong of storytelling, the scrape of the grinding stone on the sorghum grains, the bubbling of the jugs full of fermenting beer, and just by the front door, the rhythmic pounding of the pestle in the mortar. How I wish the lines I write on this page could be the path that leads me back to Stefania's house!

In Stefania's Rwanda, there are no villages. Houses are scattered over the hillsides, hidden under the thick cover of the banana trees. The enclosure – the *rugo* – is marked out by a tall ring of fig or coral trees, which support walls of interwoven reeds and bamboo. These tall hedges close off a series of half-moon shaped courtyards, set one within the next. The first is a sort of vestibule, where, as elementary courtesy demands, the visitor must announce himself and thrust his spear into the ground, or if it's a woman set down her baskets of gifts, and then await an invitation to come further. The second courtyard, the biggest, almost circular, is for the cows: they're brought in at noon, when the sun is at its hottest, and in the evening as darkness falls. Only men and virgin girls have the privilege of milking them, and they carefully collect the manure, that precious stuff, so pleasant to stick your hand into. Thick smoke from a fire of wet grass and dried manure drives away the parasites that would otherwise bedevil the herd.

The big straw dome of the *inzu*, like something erupted from the earth, sits at the far end of this main courtyard. To go inside you have to bend double, first under a sort of visor made of very carefully combed straw, then under the fat bundles of reeds or papyrus stems framing the door. When you can stand up again, your eyes have to adjust to the warm, welcoming dimness before you can make out the *inzu*'s maternal curves. 'But,' Mama used to say, 'in the *inzu*, it's not your eyes that guide you, it's your heart.' A convex screen decorated with abstract designs walls off a little antechamber where young sons sleep, often in the company of the last-born calf; other screens make a sort of alcove that hides the parents' big bed. Daughters sleep at the foot of that bed, sheltered by the screen, but the two youngest sleep with their parents, the littlest one between the mother and the wall of the *inzu*, the bigger one beside the father, who watches over the entire household within range of his spear. A long shelf – the *uruhimbi* – hugs the curve of the vaulted ceiling, and on that shelf the family's precious possessions are laid out: the milk jugs of coral-tree wood, the bulging gourds that serve as butter churns, the big baskets with their pointed lids. Under the spiral braid of the cupola, in the centre of the big basin handmade by the woman of the house, the fire crackles between the three stones of the hearth.

The back courtyard, closed off by a crescent-shaped palisade, is for storage. This is the domain of the mother of the family. She does her cooking there. She has a little garden, with a mix of medicinal plants and rare, much-prized vegetables, as well as a few tobacco plants. She and her daughters do their ablutions there. She receives her friends there. For girls of marriageable age, a smaller-sized *inzu* has been built: no man can enter, not even the father. And it was also under a simple thatched roof that they worshipped the ancestors, placing offerings in a miniature trough. In the dry season, the flamboyant blooms of the coral tree proclaimed the presence of Ryangombe, the Master of the Spirits.

Sometimes the married sons' outlying enclosures link up with the central enclosure, weaving a complicated labyrinth of fences that blur the beautiful regularity of the main *rugo*.

But of course, Stefania had no hope of building the massive enclosure I've just described. We weren't living high in the hills we'd been driven from, we were in the dry, dusty plain of the Bugesera. There were no cows to bring in every evening, and only a thin euphorbia hedge, hardly taller than Jeanne, who must just have turned five, separated us from our neighbours: neither the mayor nor the soldiers would have let us put up the high fences of the *rugo*, even if we had the means. Stefania's *inzu*, behind the Tripolo house and the banana grove, would be nothing more than – and here I have no choice but to use a word I wish I could banish – a simple hut.

But it's no small project, building an *inzu*. Especially for just two people, because Stefania had only Antoine to help her. Busy as always settling the problems of our little community of exiles, Papa was none too enthusiastic. Besides, he'd adopted some of the new ways brought by the white people. It's true that he remained ever faithful to the immaculate *pagne* that underscores the dignity of the elders (never once did I see him in trousers), but he liked the new rectangular houses, whether clay or brick. In Magi, he'd gone into debt to build a brick house, but it fell victim to the Hutus' destructive hatred before we could move in. In Gitagata, he'd put up walls inside the Tripolo house. Even Mama had joined in, plastering the walls with yellow dirt she'd gone off to gather far from the village, in the lands of the Bageseras, coating the floor with a mixture of clay and charcoal dust. 'Just like the main street in Kigali,' she liked to laugh. 'That's what they tell me! Mukasonga, isn't that exactly what asphalt looks like?' But she went on cursing that white people's house, which to her was 'a place without spirits'.

However difficult it would be, Stefania was determined to put up her *inzu*. We could call on the neighbours, of course, but only to help put it in place. Before all that the materials would have to be found, not to mention that we'd have to make enough sorghum beer and banana beer to sustain everyone's enthusiasm for the work when the big day came, and to fittingly celebrate the house's inauguration.

And so, with Stefania serving as foreman, Antoine meticulously picked out flexible branches for the armature of the thatch roof; day after day, he piled up bundles of grasses, reeds, papyrus. Then, when he'd had enough of everything, he traced the big circular footprint of the *inzu* on the ground, drove in long poles at regular intervals, and linked them together with a circular wall of interlaced bamboo.

It's the roof you need help for: the custom is to enlist your neighbours, at least ten men and as many women. Inside the bamboo wall, they weave a vault for the thatch roof to rest on. It's like a huge, widely flared basket, and when it's as big as the circle, they hoist it up on a pole, then wedge pillars beneath it – maybe ten pillars, maybe more, depending on the size of the *inzu* – to make a permanent support. Now there's nothing more to do but bend down the long branches and bind them together, then cover the whole thing with a thick blanket of thatch, carefully combed and evened out.

With that it's fair to say that the hardest work has been done, so it's time to indulge in the celebrations promised by the big jugs waiting under the banana trees. Which everyone did, of course, but even if her house wasn't as big as she wished, my mother wanted it to at least be outfitted with all the refinements required by the dignity of the family, so she went on working for a long time to make the embellishments she thought necessary. She coated the low bamboo wall of the *inzu*'s base with clay. Their little legs sunk in up to their thighs, Julienne and Jeanne trampled the mud while Alexia and I went back and forth to the lake for more water. She shaped the basin for the hearth; she wove screens, which she decorated, using black ash and cow dung that I went to fetch from the Bageseras, with beautiful motifs that to me evoked the outstretched wings of the grey crowned crane, but above all she created the endlessly long braid that, once curled into a spiral and bound to the vault, made the *inzu*'s cupola.

It was as if, thanks to her house, Stefania had regained the status and powers that Rwandan tradition ascribes to a mother. Carefully unrolling a dried, gold-tinged sorghum stem, she made herself an *urugori*, something she'd long done without, a diadem that holds up the tall hairdo worn by Rwandan women, a symbol of their fertility, a source of blessings for the children and all the family. She wore it to Mass on Sundays, and the rest of the week, when she was out working in the field, she hung it on the *uruhindu*, the little spear tip used to weave baskets, thrust for safekeeping into one of the bundles of papyrus at the entrance. The *urugori* was the sign of the maternal authority that Stefania now exercised over the *inzu* and everyone in it. When she was away, that sorghum diadem watched over her realm. At long last the grinding stone, the *urusyo*, went back to the place where it belonged: to the right of the doorway, under the papyrus arch. At the foot of the *inzu*, she reconstituted the medicinal garden that every provident mother must be forever tending and renewing. Also in its beneficial proximity, she planted the most prized and most special banana trees. And it's true that those banana trees grew so tall and vigorous that they soon submerged the house beneath their shining leaves. And then, beside the hearth, she could once again take up the thread of her tales, she could once again celebrate the exploits of King Ruganzu. Later, when I came home from high school for the holiday, it was on the doorstep that she welcomed me, softly reciting a greeting I didn't understand, but I felt sure that it placed me under the protection of the ancestral abode for as long as I stayed in Gitagata.

And the fact is that the soldiers generally spared Stefania's house; I always thought they deliberately avoided it, pretending they hadn't noticed it. To them, the *inzu* must have been the lair of fearsome spirits, whose implacable maledictions it was best to steer clear of.

On the other hand, they kept up their relentless attacks on the Tripolo house. Abandoned by Mama, it had become a sort of reception hall where Papa held court with the other village elders, where Alexia and André, the intellectuals of the family (the little table Antoine built for André wouldn't fit through the *inzu*'s narrow doorway), read on rainy days and received the occasional student from Nyamata or secondary-school friend passing through. When, thanks to his first pay cheque as a schoolteacher, André could afford a cassette player, the Tripolo house even became a dance hall, a gathering place for all the young people of Gitagata. But in spite of the danger that lurked even when there was no sign of a coming raid by the soldiers, we always ate our evening meal in that house, to take advantage of the light of the setting sun.

Stefania again became the keeper of the fire, the fire in the very centre of the *inzu*, which must never be allowed to go out. There's a whole art to keeping the fire alive for the night: every night, Mama would pull out all the unburned wood, leaving only the coals, which she covered with a layer of ash. Into that glowing pile she thrust a log that would smoulder all through the night. Before dawn – because it's shameful for sunrise to find a mother still in bed – Mama went to make sure that the embers, the seeds of the new fire, were still red under the ash. If by some misfortune they'd gone dark (and no matter how careful you are, a misfortune is always possible) you had to go borrow fire from the neighbours: you take a handful of dried grasses, you lay an ember on top of them, and you wrap it all up in a banana leaf. When you get home, you blow on the dried stems, taking great care not to let a stray spark set fire to the straw under the coffee plants. But the fire rarely went out, fortunately, because a woman who comes asking for fire from her neighbours too often is soon criticised. People say: 'That woman can't even manage to keep a fire going, she's a bad wife!'

André used to poke fun at Stefania: 'Why do you walk all over the village to find fire when we have a box of matches right at home?' Because along with the vial of Lourdes water and the pair of glasses for reading the Bible, the Fathers had given Papa, as head of the Legion of Mary, a box of matches. I don't know if they ever gave him a second one. 'Listen to me, my son,' Mama would sigh, 'the white people have given us so many gifts, and look where it's gotten us! So, when I have to, let me go looking for fire just as we've always done here. At least that's one thing we have left.'

SORGHUM

People have sometimes described Tutsi women as airy aristocrats whose only occupations are weaving quaint little baskets or lazily rocking a big calabash with a prettily arched neck on their outstretched legs, churning the beauty butter that gave those vestals of the source of the Nile the glistening, satiny skin that so fascinated the Europeans. I myself always saw my mother with her hoe in her hand, tilling the soil, sowing, weeding, harvesting, both before our exile, in Gikongoro, in Magi, and even more afterwards in Nyamata, in the deportees' villages. Because in Rwanda the work in the fields never ends. It begins, if a beginning must be found for what in fact has no beginning or end, with the first rains in October, when beans and corn are planted, to be harvested in December and

February respectively; then comes the main rainy season, from March to May, the time to sow sorghum, which will be harvested in July, at the start of the dry season. But meanwhile there are also the beans to be tended, and sweet potatoes, eleusine, taro, squash, yams, manioc, and especially the banana grove. Rwandan women like Stefania, like all of them today, Tutsis and Hutus alike, do not spend their days weaving those dainty nesting baskets that so many tourists see as their principal activity.

Sorghum had a special place among our crops. It had its own special dignity. It didn't mingle with the others. It needed its own plot, a field all to itself. Taro, sweet potatoes, beans, all those vegetables could live together perfectly well. The bean vines clung to the cornstalks, and the sweet potatoes and taro sheltered under the banana tree, and none of them ever complained. Which isn't to say that we took beans, sweet potatoes, or corn for granted. Without them, what would we have eaten? How to satisfy a Rwandan's appetite without his daily plate of beans? I was greatly surprised when I heard sweet potatoes, corn, and beans had come to us from America. What roads had those plants taken to get all the way to Rwanda? I never heard an answer. In any case, our grandparents didn't need agronomists or experts from the FAO. They got along all by themselves, without waiting for someone to come show them how to farm their own field.

But sorghum was a true Rwandan. Its field was like its enclosure. You couldn't bring just anything into it. We did sometimes try to plant sweet potatoes – *impungine* – at its feet. But we knew that was wrong, that it showed a lack of respect for the sorghum. And so, not wanting to disturb it, we pretended to forget the sweet potatoes were there. Left in the ground for too long, they grew so huge that they lost all their taste and put us all off. And of course many of them rotted. The sorghum would not stand for those trespassers.

Sorghum was the king of our fields. There was a whole ceremony to farming it, and even to eating it, rituals that Stefania performed with loving piety, because sorghum was a plant of good omen: a fine field of sorghum was a talisman against famine and calamity, a sign of fertility and abundance, and for us children a generous purveyor of treats and games.

Sorghum is sown just before the main rainy season, which runs from March to May. Everyone hopes the rain will keep the appointment, but they always fear its sudden caprices. And so, once she'd ploughed the ground with a hoe, Mama threw out big handfuls of seeds, some of them white sorghum, which she'd use for porridge and paste, and some red, which was reserved for beer. She hoed the ground again to bury the seeds in the dirt. With my little hoe, I imitated my mother's movements. It was tiring to stay bent over like that all day long. Mama heard my groans. 'Oh, Mukasonga,' she would say to me, not even turning around, 'you've got nothing to complain about, wait till you see what it's like hoeing with a baby on your back!' Worms slithered under my feet. Some of them were as big as small snakes, and I didn't much care for them. But Mama expressed her delight: 'Good soil we've got here! I didn't go wrong when I picked out this field, just look at all those worms! Don't kill them, they're not slugs, they mean us well: they're the sign of a good harvest!' And it's true, the sorghum grew profusely, and so we had to thin the field, keep it weeded.

Clearing the field of weeds and interlopers is a slow, painstaking process. It takes close attention but not a great deal of energy. There's plenty of opportunity to talk and tell stories. It was while we were weeding the sorghum field that Mama taught me most of her memories of the Rwanda that used to be. Alas! I've forgotten so many of the secrets Stefania told me, the secrets a mother tells only her daughter.

If the soil was fertile, if the rain was abundant, the sorghum grew quickly. Jeanne, Julienne, and I measured ourselves by its stalks; before long they were little-girl sized, and then they were as tall as our parents. Soon they were bigger than people, bigger than Sekimonyo, the beekeeper, who could hang his hives in the tallest branches of the trees without straining. We watched for the flowers to bloom, we looked at the seed heads slowly taking shape in their leafy cloaks. Some were red and some white. But it wasn't the red or white panicles that interested the children, it was the *inopfu*, the sterile sorghum plants, the ones that never make seeds. Those unwelcome intruders' green leaves concealed not seeds but a white, shapeless mass, striped with black filaments. That was what we coveted, *inopfu*, like a bar of black and white chocolate offered to children by the sorghum. Much to my parents' dismay, we wished the whole field would produce nothing but *inopfu*. No such luck: *inopfu* were rare, and to spot them you had to get far away, you had to climb a termite mound or a little hill with a bird's eye view of the field. Two little plumes, a bit like the horns of a giant snail, signalled the presence of an *inopfu*. Quick as we could, we three wriggled our way between the stalks, taking great pains not to break them, so we could harvest that strange fruit of sterility. When we emerged from among the towering sorghum plants, the black streaks on our lips and tongues showed everyone that the hunting was good.

Sorghum is harvested in July, at the start of the dry season. But before that, when the heads have already formed but the grains aren't quite dry yet, my mother celebrated *Umuganura*. *Umuganura* is the name of the festival and also of the sorghum paste you have to eat for the occasion.

There was no question of harvesting before the whole family had eaten the first sorghum paste, in accordance with the ritual. No ethnologist had told us that what we were doing was celebrating the first fruits of the harvest, but we knew that *Umuganura* marked the start of a new year, that this was the time to make wishes so the year ushered in by the sorghum would bring us good fortune. Back then, we knew nothing of the white people's New Year's Day.

Umuganura was a family festival. Not even the neighbours were invited. Everyone celebrated it in the privacy of their own enclosure, away from the others. Maybe that's why it had escaped the missionaries' censure: they never even tried to Christianise it. And so, thanks to the mothers, sorghum put up a quiet resistance in every home.

To make *umuganura*, you had to collect the grains when they were still swollen with water, just enough to make the paste, no more. It was generally one of the children of the house who had the honour of gathering the panicles. And not just any child: not illegitimate, obviously, but also not sickly or stunted, no child with the slightest physical defect. Stefania always assigned that ritual harvest to me. She didn't have a choice. André and Alexia were in school, they were 'evolved', and though they didn't show it too openly they found Stefania's strange liturgies faintly ridiculous. Jeanne was too little, and Mama thought of Julienne as a fragile child, in precarious health. Following Mama's instructions,

I chose the seed heads that were heaviest with grains, the ones that foretold an abundant harvest and a year that we hoped would be prosperous in spite of everything. Very respectfully, I laid them in a basket specially woven for the purpose. The metal pots and basins sold in the market were strictly forbidden for *umuganura*.

Those swollen grains aren't ground on the millstone like ordinary sorghum, but crushed in the mortar. On a winnowing basket, smeared with a fresh coating of manure a few weeks before, we picked out the ones that hadn't been crushed and put them back in the mortar until we had the finest possible flour. Mama made the paste in a clay pot – at every stage of the process, we had to avoid all utensils brought by the white people. The recipe? I think it's more or less the same as for the buckwheat galettes they make in Brittany, but Stefania wasn't making crêpes: little by little she mixed the flour with boiling water until she had a beautiful ball, a perfect sphere, very smooth, prettily flecked with pale green. And all the while she spoke formulas I never quite understood, but which I heard as a curse on poisoners and sorcerers and a plea for fertility, plenty, and fecundity for the family, the enclosure, the fields, and especially the herd of cows we didn't have.

The main ritual took place at night, by the light of a full moon. The entire family was supposed to taste the *umuganura*, to taste the new year announced by the coming sorghum harvest. Mama set the ball of paste in a little basket reserved for that ceremony alone, and, with a blade of stiff, sharp-edged swamp grass, *urutamyi*, a reed used for basketry, she cut off a piece for each one of us. Nothing metal, not a knife, not even a spoon, could be allowed to touch the *umuganura*. Once that was done, Stefania again spoke the incantations, which we then had to repeat in chorus, replacing for that one evening the prayer Papa made us recite before every meal. The time had come to eat the *umuganura*. I swallowed it as reverently as I did the holy wafers the Fathers put on my tongue. The *umuganura* paste seemed to me perfectly exquisite, compared to the everyday paste that crunched between your teeth, scraped your throat, plugged up your stomach, the paste Mama forced us to choke down in spite of our spirited objections. A jug of beer was awaiting us, and there was nothing left to do but sing and dance in the sorghum's honour. And so we did, deep into the night.

Harvest time comes. There's not a moment to waste. The birds are holding an enormous conclave all around the field. For once the monkeys are no cause for concern: they take no interest in sorghum. But in Rwanda, even in the Bugesera, you mustn't place too much faith in the dry season. The rain could be coming. And indeed that dreaded rain has a name all its own: nothing other than 'sorghum rain'.

Before the harvest, you have to make a threshing floor. We no longer have the big mat people had 'in Rwanda', a mat used for this occasion alone, broad enough to completely cover the back courtyard; in the Bugesera the only choice is to coat a part of the yard with cow manure. We have to go and ask for that manure from the Bageseras, since we destitute refugees have no cows. Luckily for us, the Bageseras know nothing about business: they give away their herd's droppings and ask for nothing in return. Not even that sudden surge in demand could push them to seek a profit from what they had. The market economy had yet to come to the Bugesera. It's true that Julienne and I often simply followed the cows and collected their dung without asking anyone's permission. Parades of women and girls walked the dirt roads of the Bugesera, proudly sporting baskets of manure on their heads. That dung is then spread over the courtyard, and we take the opportunity to smear it on our winnows and baskets so they'll be perfectly sealed. But an unexpected rain is always to be feared, so every family weaves a sort of bed, like the parents' bed but higher and wider, which the seed heads can quickly be shovelled onto before the rain turns the threshing floor into foul-smelling puddles and streams.

Cutting the sorghum is men's work. In fact, it's the work of all the men in the village. They come together and mow the fields one by one. You have to be quick when the seed heads are ready, quicker than the birds, quicker than the rain that could come at any moment. And in the evening, everyone – men, women, and children – gathers around the jugs of the family whose field was just mown. The sorghum harvest is a fine time.

Still on the stalks, the seed heads are left to lie in the field for two or three days before they're cut off. Now it's the women's and children's turn to work. Needless to say, you can count on the neighbour women to help: they know you'll soon be labouring beside them in their own fields. The children's job is to carry the panicles to the threshing floor, or to the granary that's been built if the harvest promises to be bounteous. They run all the way, the baskets on their heads. It's not a chore. Everyone volunteers. The schoolteacher knows the classroom will sit empty on those days. The children are zealous workers: they can already taste the reward that awaits them at the end of the day – the *imisigati*! Sorghum never forgets the children: in a few of its stalks – not all of them, to our regret – it's secretly stored up a sugary juice, sweeter than honey. During the harvest, those coveted *imisigati* have been carefully picked out and set aside, kept cool in the shade of the banana grove. Mama has even buried a few of them, awaiting the return of André and Alexia. But this evening *imisigati* will be handed out to all the little workers. The fattest go to the most deserving children, the ones who most conscientiously filled their baskets, who ran fastest back and forth. My lazy niece Muberejiki earns just one single, skinny stalk. Everyone gathers under the banana trees to chew at the stalks and suck down their heavenly sap. Even the mamas join in, taking their share of that delectable *imisigati* syrup.

Once the seed heads have been threshed, there's a mountain of grain in the courtyard. The children play at sinking into it like quicksand. The mamas keep a close eye on the little ones who crawl onto the pile, for fear an avalanche might bury them alive.

Sorghum was used for making paste, the paste we so loathed, that Mama forced us to eat. You could also drop the grain into boiling water, like you were making rice, but that was only in times of famine. There was also *agacoma*, a porridge, like very thick soup. *Agacoma* was considered a tonic, and was given to children instead of milk, to convalescents, to women in labour, to old people. Happy were the aged parents who could say, 'I'm lucky, I haven't been abandoned, my daughter still brings me *agacoma*!' Stefania made it for André and Alexia when they were home in Gitagata. She brought them big calabashes of piping hot porridge as soon as they were up in the morning. 'How ashamed I would be,' she often said, 'if my children went back to school thinner than when they came home to me!'

Of course, what everyone was most eagerly awaiting from the sorghum was beer. Sorghum beer: this was back before Primus and Amstel relegated it to the unloved ranks of archaic libations old people still force you to share, an invitation you don't dare refuse. Sorghum beer was the very foundation of conviviality for all Rwandans. Family bonds were strengthened around the beer jug, friendships were born or revived, neighbourly relationships affirmed, marriages negotiated, quarrels calmed, conflicts resolved; and the sage, having plunged his straw into the thick foam and taken a long sip of the brownish liquid, spoke just the right proverb to illuminate the situation and decide the proper course of action to pursue.

The first thing you need to make sorghum beer is a great many vessels. You gather up all you own – the trough that's also used for banana beer, the big urns for storing rainwater. In later times, after civilisation gradually made its way across the Nyabarongo, the villagers would take up a collection to buy one of the big metal cans they had at the market in Nyamata – a jerrican, as the evolved people called it, a container for the palm oil the shop-keepers parcelled out in broken Fanta bottles. Common property, that precious can made the rounds from family to family. You pour the grains into the trough, the jugs, or the jerrican, along with enough water to cover them. You let the sorghum steep for four days until it's thoroughly soaked and the grains go soft. In the meantime, you line the threshing floor with big banana leaves, choosing only the most perfect ones, with no holes or tears, so you'll have a thick, flawless carpet. You burn *amashara*, dried banana leaves, which will give you a very black ash. You spread the sorghum grains over the carpet of leaves and cover it all with ash, mixing it in until the sorghum's very black, which gives you what's known as *amamera*. You let the grains sprout beneath a layer of banana leaves, and soon they're covered with white filaments. Then you have to let them dry in the sun. When the grains are ready, the women get down on their knees and the children on all fours to rub off the sprouts; they take advantage of the occasion to stuff themselves with sweet, black grain, yet another of sorghum's many treats! You winnow the grains, then crush them on the grinding stone (never with the mortar and pestle!) and the flour is stored up in the big baskets with pointed lids set out in the place of honour on the *uruhimbi*, the shelf that runs along the curve of the *inzu*. Those baskets will be dipped into when beer-making day comes.

Making sorghum beer doesn't take long: just a day and a night. You put the flour in the trough, you pour boiling water over it, and you stir with a spatula the size of an oar. What you want is a clear, pale, sweet gruel. You divide that among the jugs, adding a little yeast – *umusemburo* – that you get from plants gathered in the bush (don't bother asking, it's a secret) and you go to sleep listening to the beer bubble and sigh as it ferments in the big black jugs at the foot of the parents' bed.

Now there's nothing left in the fields but the cut stalks, long gone dry. They're not useless, as you might think. Those are used to renovate, reinforce, or patch fences, and also to make *mahubusi* – scarecrows – that will, at least for a while, keep the pillaging monkeys away from the sweet potatoes. Those sweet potatoes have to be protected, because when the dry season comes there's nothing else to eat in the fields.

Mothers who farm with their babies on their backs also need the dried sorghum stalks. When the baby gets too heavy, it has to be put down beneath a shelter the mama builds at the edge of the field. She makes a frame out of stalks, then covers it with fresh grasses. She carefully lines the inside with banana leaves and weaves a little raised cradle, inaccessible to snakes. Then she can go back to her field: the baby is well protected from the sun and the sharp eyes of the birds of prey watching from high above.

The sorghum still had one last gift for the children; for them, there was always something more. The long school holiday began just after the harvest, and the fallow field offered both girls and boys an endless variety of games all through the dry season. With great skill and even greater imagination, we transformed those dry stalks into all sorts of prized objects, as coveted as they were unattainable. First among them were glasses, like the Fathers wore. I knew all about glasses; Papa had a pair, as I've said, even if he never put them on at home except for reading the Bible. But he was the only one in the village. Many people thought they were reserved for missionaries, that with their glasses they could read our thoughts, search the very depths of our souls for the sins we were trying to hide from them. As etiquette dictated, we girls bowed our heads to avoid the stares they gave us from behind their glasses, but the boys were bolder; they wanted glasses of their own. So they looked closely at those glasses, they studied them. That wasn't easy – at Mass the priest kept his back to you, and when he turned around to say the service was over he was too far away. You had to wait for him to come observe the catechism lesson given to us after school by Rukema, the deacon. The boys kept their eyes glued to the missionary, who praised them for their attentiveness, but it wasn't the Father's words that interested them, it was his glasses!

The boys were proud: now they knew how to make glasses. They cut two thin rounds of bark from the sorghum stalk, then two little rods for the arms, and stuck it all together with soft, white pith from inside the stalks. The lack of lenses didn't bother anyone; it was the frames that mattered. The boys walked around gravely, sticking their stomachs out, those sorghum glasses precariously balanced on their noses, and we hailed them, laughing: '*Abapadri! Abapadri!*'

We girls made dolls by cutting up the sorghum's soft pith, a round piece for the head, a cylinder for the body, little rolled pieces for the arms and legs, three sorghum grains for the nose and eyes. A few twigs pulled from the stalk made a skeleton. But that sorghum baby was missing the most important thing: glasses! Only the boldest girls dared try to borrow them from the boys.

MEDICINE

It took us some time, when we were first in Nyamata, crammed into the classrooms of the primary school, to discover that there was a dispensary nearby. Many of the displaced people weren't well, what with the strange food handed out to us, and the heat of the Bugesera, so difficult to tolerate for us mountain folk from Butare, and then the lack of milk, which for many had always been the essential food, and the cramped quarters, the lack of hygiene ... Dysentery began to spread, and among the elderly and the very small children there were more than a few deaths. At the far end of the dusty schoolyard where the families had resigned themselves to putting up their huts, there was a dilapidated old colonial building: the dispensary. The nurse was a Tutsi from Butare, like us.

He'd preceded us into exile. His name was Bitega, and he was widely given the title of doctor – *muganga*. Before long the sick and the curious were lining up before the sheet-metal-roofed porch where Bitega officiated. They were soon disappointed. Bitega had only two medicines to prescribe: aspirin and cough syrup. There was one day for aspirin and one day for syrup. The syrup was sweet. Syrup day was the children's day. I waited with all the others, I opened my mouth wide when my turn came, and at long last Bitega's boy stuck in the single spoon that dispensed syrup to all of us. Many there were who tried to get back into line for a second spoonful. But there was no fooling Bitega: he recognised the cheaters without a moment's hesitation.

Exploring the little village's few streets, Papa and his friends spotted another colonial house, as run-down as the dispensary, behind the market square. They made the acquaintance of the occupant: a veterinarian, Gatashya, who looked after cows. That news caused a sensation. A man who knew how to care for cows, the most precious possession imaginable, was surely all the more skilled in treating human beings. And so the lines that formed every morning in front of Bitega's dispensary moved to the covered terrace, the 'barza' as the Belgian colonists called it, of the veterinarian Gatashya. But Gatashya was a wise man. He had limited faith in his own drugs, and he advised the ailing to use medicinal plants instead.

That was Stefania's opinion, too. She didn't believe in Bitega's syrup and pills. She was sorry she'd lost the means to concoct the traditional remedies – the only ones, she assured us, that could combat the illnesses that afflicted Rwandans, particularly children. And so, as soon she could, first in Gitwe and then especially in Gitagata, she set about rebuilding her botanical pharmacy. It extended all the way around the house, and it had everything she might need for her unguents and decoctions.

Stefania wasn't one of those healers people come to for serious cases, with high hopes and deep trepidation, but like most Rwandan women she knew of many medications, which she mixed and applied herself, mindful of the case at hand, with conviction, and most often, I believe, with success. Her pharmacopoeia was made up of the grasses, tubers, roots, and tree leaves of the savannah. To anyone clearing a field, she pointed out all the plants worth saving, and in her medicinal garden she planted the ones she would use for her cures.

Like any good mother, Mama had all kinds of remedies against the illnesses and injuries that would inevitably befall her family as the days went by.

For small burns, it was simple: all she had to do was spit on the burned skin and most importantly speak the formula *Pfuba nk'ubwanwa bw'umugore* – 'May the burn not come out, like a beard [doesn't come out] on a woman.' There was also sticky *uruteja* sap or crushed potato, but potatoes were for rich people – we didn't grow them in Nyamata, they came from Ruhengeri, from the fertile land at the foot of the volcanoes, so fertile that some potatoes could grow as big as melons. Oh, those *intofanyi* of Ruhengeri! We country children admired them from afar when we were in the city on an errand and had to pay a call on some high functionary. Now and then, despite the reluctance of Madame and the houseboys, we were shown into the living room of his villa: there they were, those potatoes, the celebrated *intofanyi*, sitting behind the mosquito netting draped over the cooler people commonly used as a sideboard, very visibly displayed in their 'Made in Hong Kong' dish decorated with red flowers. Still glistening with the frying oil, those potatoes bore witness to this important personage's wealth, and tormented the little visitor's appetite.

No part of the body was more prone to wounds than the feet. We never wore shoes, and when we came home from school and still had to fetch water or dry wood, nightfall – which in Rwanda comes at six o'clock year-round – often caught us on the road home. In the dark, and since we had to stand up very straight to keep the jug or bundled twigs on our heads, we were constantly stubbing our toes on small rocks, scraping them in the potholes. By the time I got home, my feet were bleeding, the nails broken or torn. When Alexia was with me, she always came back without a scratch on her feet, as if she'd glided over all the dirt road's ruts and sharp stones. Mama used to say, 'Alexia has eyes in her toes. You and Julienne' – because Julienne's feet were in the same state as mine – 'your toes are blind, but I'll teach them to see.' And so, after the evening meal, in pitch darkness, Stefania tried to teach our toes how to see. She made a torch of dry branches and swept the flame over the ground just before our feet. She harangued our toes, particularly the big toe, the most exposed to the dangers of the road. 'Open your eyes, and from now on may you see in the dark, may you know your way.' But like mine, Julienne's toes stubbornly went on seeing nothing; their eyes refused to open. Mama wouldn't give up. 'When you walk,' she advised us, 'you have to talk to your heart, because it's the heart that spreads light all through your body. So tell it to remind your toes that they have to watch where you're stepping, and it will tell them, "It's dark out. Open your eyes. I'll look straight ahead; you look down."' But it was no use, our toes wouldn't listen. We had to start the ritual all over again, give it more time. We went out into the yard, we walked the little path to the road. Bent double, Mama walked backwards in front of us: the flames of her torch nearly licked at our feet. Some evenings we even ventured into the bush, seeking out the darkest spot, where, Stefania hoped, our toes' eyes would have no choice but to open. Alas, neither Stefania's exhortations nor her torch nor the darkness of the bush could convince our toes to open their eyes. They were closed for all time. Mama worried over our future: 'With feet like yours,' she would sigh, 'I wonder who'll want anything to do with you when you're old enough to marry.'

I can't help thinking that the curse my mother couldn't dispel still hangs over my toes, and I always dread having to buy new shoes: I suspect the saleswoman (and sometimes even the other customers) of staring at my feet, at best in surprise, but more often with repugnance or scorn. Thank goodness for tights: they cover many flaws.

No less common, especially for girls, were the wounds you could give yourself in the field, working the soil. It was so easy to slice into your leg or foot with the hoe. My mother's prescription was to quickly pack the wound with dirt, not the dry, dusty dirt under your feet but the dark, moist dirt that imparts life to seeds; later, if need be, the wound could be daubed with *umutumba*, a sort of pith found in the stumps of banana trees. If the wound still wouldn't heal, the next step was to dry the leaves of a *nkuyimwonga*, a plant with mauve flowers, pulverise them on the grinding stone, and cover the wound with the powder.

If the wound became infected, stronger measures were required. Foremost among them was *kalifuma*, a mysterious yellow powder said to come from Zanzibar. You bought it from the *magendu*. That was what we called itinerant pharmacists who hawked all sorts of drugs and medications – every one of them from Zanzibar, they assured us. But for desperate cases, there was still *muriro*, fire. That too you bought from the *magendu*. It was a blue stone that you ground down little by little, as you needed it. When you put it on the wound, the pain was excruciating, it was like fire. *Muriro* was only to be used when it seemed there was nothing else to be done. Just hearing its name filled you with terror!

Mama used it once, I remember, for Muberejiki, one of my older sister Judith's daughters. The little girl, who might have been three years old, had a deep cut on her ankle. Gangrene was feared. When she saw her condition, my mother immediately decided there was no time to waste, that only *muriro* could heal her, and without it she would lose her whole leg. But before she sprinkled the powder on the wound, my mother crossed herself again and again, all the while invoking the great Master of the Spirits, Ryangombe, whom the Fathers described as the devil himself: *Ryangombe rya ya data! Ryangombe rya data!* 'Ryangombe, god of our fathers!' Frightened out of our minds, Julienne and I stopped up our ears so we wouldn't hear Muberejiki screaming as Antoine struggled to hold her still. I think I can still hear those screams today . . .

Did Muberejiki owe her recovery to the fiery force of the *muriro* or to Ryangombe's therapeutic omnipotence? That I can't say.

But Mama's daily concern, like every other Rwandan mother's, was the intestinal worms she believed to be sapping her children's fragile health. To Stefania, a swollen stomach – most likely caused by malnutrition – was the unmistakable symptom of those elusive parasites' presence. She used *umubirizi* leaves as a vermifuge. You always had to have an *umubirizi* plant close by, because it was effective against many illnesses. When you built a house, the first thing you had to plant was *umubirizi*, along with *umuravumba*, another reputed panacea. You extracted the juice from the green *umubirizi* leaves by rubbing them between your hands. Diluted in a little water, it made a very bitter potion. It might have been from that disagreeable taste that *umubirizi* got its reputation as a miracle cure. Children lived in terror of the day when they would be prescribed a dose of *umubirizi*. The mothers kept a close watch over the little calabash that held the vermifuge, forever fearing a poisoner might creep near the precious remedy.

But inevitably, in the never-ending battle against those invisible enemies, the child would require an enema. For that the mothers would pick a fairly common climbing plant, *umunkamba*, steep it, strain the liquid. Then they'd need a nozzle, which wasn't hard to find: all you had to do was cut the hollow stem of a squash. Once it's peeled, like an asparagus stalk, that flexible tube goes into the baby's bottom as soft as can be. The mother takes a mouthful of vermifuge; she blows it through the stem and waits for the honey-coloured spray to spatter her face, much to her delight. That's the proof that the vermifuge worked.

In no way are these procedures sheltered from prying eyes. Quite the contrary, enema day is an excuse for a lively get-together among the women. It's also a Sunday-afternoon entertainment. The mamas gather in the back courtyard as the sun begins to set. They fashion aprons from big banana leaves. Children under six are lined up by size, and they await their turn with some apprehension. The mothers feel each child's stomach to determine the appropriate dose of vermifuge: you need a good pair of lungs to deal with the ones whose hard bellies are as taut as a bowstring. The mothers laugh and congratulate each other when a brown spurt splashes their green aprons.

Among all the miseries of deportation and exile, the inability to care for their children as they were used to doing, as they'd always seen their mothers do, was not the least of the women's torments. Those salutary *umubirizi* leaves were obviously nowhere to be found in the dusty Nyamatan schoolyard, and the dry bush of the Bugesera offered only unfamiliar plants whose virtues and dangers they knew nothing about. In the villages, in Gitwe, in Gitagata, they first had to find enough food to fend off star-vation before they could go back to planting and tending the simples and gourds that constituted their natural pharmacy. The mothers were desperate. Their children's bellies were aswarm with little snakes devouring them from inside. Their health would surely be permanently affected, and as long as she lived Mama was convinced that Julienne, born in the classroom at Nyamata and deprived of the life-saving enemas, would suffer frail health forever.

But a strange tool was handed from family to family: an *umupila*. In Kinyarwanda, the word *umupila* is used for any object that has no fixed shape: a balloon, an inner tube, a pullover sweater. In this, case, the *umupila* was an enema bulb. Maybe a Father from the mission had given it to someone, maybe an evolved mother had bought it in one of the handful of shops at the Nyamata marketplace, where she found it lying between a few packs of cigarettes and four bottles of orange Fanta, unsold and unsellable. The enema bulb met with little success. My mother refused point blank to use the thing, whose hard tip would surely injure a baby's sensitive, delicate skin. Furthermore, with the *umupila* they wouldn't feel the procedure's result on their bodies, and without that how could you be a real mother?

When André, home from school, tried to push a more *civilised* way of doing things on Stefania, she answered: '*Musemakweri!* Aren't you my son? What can you teach me? Didn't I eat your caca?'

Baby caca, yellow as a sparrow's, was called *ubunyano*. It was important for the bonds it created, not just between mother and child, but also between the newborn and all the children of the village. *Ubunyano* was also the name of a festival celebrated just after the baby's birth, its first time out of the house. A sort of ceremony to mark the mother's rising, but most of all a party for the neighbourhood children.

I took part only once, at the house of our neighbour Marie-Thérèse, who'd given birth to a boy after so many girls. Mama didn't approve of those festivities. She found them 'too pagan'. Not to mention that she couldn't stand to see her own children eating the neighbour's baby's caca, even if it was more or less symbolically: caca was a private matter, between a mother and her child. Still, there was no refusing an invitation from such a nearby neighbour, and so, before I went to the party, Mama gave me a long list of instructions, which could be summed up as follows: 'Whatever you do, don't touch anything!'

The morning of the party, all the women gathered at the new mother's to make the meal the children would be offered that evening. There were beans, and especially sweet potatoes – the best ones, with white, mealy flesh. The party, the *Ubunyano*, was held in the evening, when the sun glowed red at the very bottom of the sky, before it disappeared behind the banana trees. Then all the children of Gitagata headed toward Marie-Thérèse's house. We sat down on mats laid out in a circle in the courtyard. Our mamas stood behind us. There were no men; the *Ubunyano* wasn't their affair. There was a bigger mat in the middle of the circle of women and children. We waited. After a long while – I believe it was after the moon had come up – Marie-Thérèse and her baby appeared and took their place on that big central mat. She presented her baby to the gathered children and women of the village, and even those who'd already seen him, who'd helped with the delivery, pretended they were beholding him for the very first time, and made a great fuss over him. We'd been told it's the moon that gives newborns their hair, and on that child's head it had left only a crescent, exactly in its image.

Then, on the big basket used for winnowing sorghum, they brought out the beans, the sweet potatoes, and beneath that steaming, delectable-smelling dinner lay – so we'd been convinced – all the caca that had come out of the baby since its birth. Which was why, in a grave violation of good manners, we were supposed to plunge our hands deep into the tempting mound. The children vaguely understood that to taste the new arrival's *ubunyano* was to welcome him into our midst, to recognise him as a brother we had to protect, and help to grow up, and teach how to escape all the mortal dangers hanging over him because like us he was unlucky enough to have been born a Tutsi.

I never found out if there really was a dollop of Marie-Thérèse's baby's faeces under the beans and sweet potatoes. In any case, that did nothing to dampen the children's vigorous appetite. I myself didn't dare reach for the *ubun-yano* like the others. I knew Mama's reproachful eye was on me, and it was with resignation and regret that I watched my companions feast to their hearts' content.

Once the big basket was picked clean, the children – the little girls, that is, because boys are always considered too clumsy – were given permission to sit down with Marie-Thérèse and her baby. They stretched out their legs and held out their arms to take him, one by one. Alas, I wasn't allowed to hold Marie-Thérèse's baby in my arms: they didn't trust me, I'd broken too many calabashes fetching water.

The next day Marie-Thérèse put her baby on her back and proudly brought him from house to house, then set off to farm her field. From now on the baby could leave the enclosure: he'd been adopted by the entire village.

Nonetheless, in spite of all the plants whose powers she knew, all the incantations she could speak just when they were needed, all the *magendu*'s exotic drugs, Mama was convinced we lacked the true life source that protects you from both illness and sorrow, that immunises you against poisons, that wards off bad spells . . . I'm talking, of course, about milk, *amata*, the supreme wealth and joy of the cow owner! No doubt it was in a spirit of derision – simply speaking the name left a bitter taste in our mouths – that we'd been deported to Nyamata: *nya-amata*, the land of milk! A place of the bleakest sterility, where the Bageseras' scrawny herds were slowly dying out from illness and thirst.

They'd killed all our cows, and burned the calves in the stables. Can you still be a man if you don't have a herd? And what do you do with your days if you don't lead your cows to their pastures, if you don't call each one by its name, if you don't smooth down their coats with a handful of soft grasses, if you don't inspect their hooves for pebbles and thorns, if you don't murmur flattering words into the ear of your favourite heifer, if you don't sing her praises before gatherings of your fellow men? How can you seal a friendship without the promise of a cow? How can you marry off your son if you don't have a perfect heifer to offer as dowry? And can you be proud of your *inzu* if the sour smell of old milk and rancid butter doesn't hang in the air, if the mother of the family isn't swinging the pot-bellied churn?

Mama sent Julienne and me to buy milk from the Bageseras. For that, we had to sell the finest bunches of bananas at the market. We brought back the milk – oh, so little milk! – in a little black jug used for butter, because of course we no longer had our pots of coral-tree wood, the only containers truly worthy of that precious liquid. Mama had us swallow a mouthful, and then she did the same, leaving just a bit in the bottom of the little pot. She set it at the foot of the parental bed, on a carpet of fine grasses, *ishinge*, and every morning, before the little pot with its few drops of milk, she prayed that that elixir of life would protect our family.

BREAD

In Nyamata, bread was thought of as medicine more than anything else. A remedy given to gravely ill children, as a last resort, when all the other treatments had been tried – enemas, plants from the medicinal garden or the bush, drugs from the *magendu*, even rice and tea, those rare, exotic products brought by the white people and reputed to work miraculous cures. If none of those had any effect, if no improvement could be seen, then there was nothing more to give the little dying child but bread. But there was no bread in Nyamata. You had to go and get it in Kigali, so Papa set off for the capital. It's not a short trip, two days going, two days coming back. In Kigali, Papa didn't go and buy bread from the bakery run by the Greeks. That bread was for white people and their houseboys, who lined up first thing in the morning for their bosses' breakfast tartines and brioches. Buying the Greeks' bread would have taken a good part of our earnings from the coffee harvest. Papa went to the market, where women sold bread they made themselves. Little round loaves, not much bigger than your fist, as pasty and sticky as manioc. Papa didn't haggle. You don't haggle over the bread that's going to cure your child. He bought four little loaves and started straight back for Nyamata, firmly hoping that precious bread would save the little patient.

One day, however, bread finally came to Nyamata. It was brought by Nyirabazungu, 'the-woman-of-the-white-people', also known as Kilimadame, the Almost-Madame. As her name tells you, Nyirabazungu worked in Kigali among the Bazungu, the white people. She looked after Madame's children. But – if I can say this of a woman – she had more than one arrow in her quiver. The proof is that she had many children of unknown fathers, being raised by her aged mother in Nyamata. The villagers took a dim view of that, since such children are always thought to bring bad luck.

With all her many and varied activities, Nyirabazungu had managed to save up some money, which she used to come and settle in Nyamata. She caused quite a stir. The men, by which I mean the town functionaries and teachers with a little money, had eyes only for her. The upright mothers were offended by her freewheeling ways, which they predicted would soon endanger more than one household. We little girls wholeheartedly admired her walk and her dress. It was as if all of Kigali had found its way into our midst. Like her, we wiggled our little bottoms, which obviously couldn't compete with her prominent posterior. We envied her colourful *pagnes*, her high-heeled shoes. But there was no imitating the way she tied her scarf on her head, in a style called *sinabwana*, she-who-has-no-man. Yes, that was her, Kilimadame, the Almost-Madame! Because while we were convinced that only a white woman could be called Madame, we Nyamatans could be proud: we had our own Almost-Madame!

Kilimadame opened a shop on the market square in Nyamata, which like all the others sold beer – the incomparable Primus – and orange Fanta, lemon Fanta, packs of cigarettes, soap ... But Kilimadame's shop, and this was a revolution in Nyamata, also sold bread. Kilimadame had learnt to make bread by watching the women in the Kigali market. She built an oven behind her shop, and into its glowing maw she put the pallid little balls of dough that came out beautifully browned, the colour of dry grass. Candida and I loved to watch as Kilimadame busily kneaded the dough, pulled it and stretched it, formed the little loaves. We weren't the only ones. There was always a crowd of children sitting around Kilimadame's oven, and when she took out the loaves they kept their eyes glued to that bread they wouldn't be eating, but whose sight alone transported them to another world, beyond the Nyabarongo, a happier world they couldn't be part of.

Kilimadame's shop prospered. It expanded, became a 'hotel'. In Rwanda a hotel isn't a place with rooms to sleep in; it's a bar that serves beer, brochettes, and even, from time to time, 'civilised' food, which means food cooked with palm oil. The men of the village – the important ones – congregate there after dark. All evening long they tell and retell the same village tales, they discuss the latest news from the capital. Often it's boring. But if you really want to be a man, someone who matters in the village, you have to be there. Thanks to Kilimadame, Nyamata was making great strides toward civilisation, but those innovations nearly shattered the solidarity the displaced community had so long shown, and introduced discord and suspicion even into the hearts of the families.

Among the displaced people, buyers of bread were of course few and far between. They were the teachers, and the ones – you could count them on one hand – who'd married their daughters to white people, and the ones who were lucky enough to have a son or daughter who'd stayed behind and found work. Proud were the children of those privileged few. They ate their loaves of bread in front of us all, slowly, taking their time, making a great show of chewing it, refusing to share or offer so much as a few crumbs to their friends, who, angry and miserable, pretended not to be watching. On top of that, Kilimadame's hotel cast suspicion on all the men who volunteered to go sell a bundle of dry wood or a bunch of bananas in the Nyamata market. Would they really bring home all their earnings, as a good father must do, or would they waste a hefty share of it at Kilimadame's, drinking beer, eating a brochette for all to see, and maybe – the height of gluttony and selfishness – savouring a loaf of bread all alone! Stefania kept a close eye on the men of Gitagata. Some she placed in the shameful category of 'gourmands', a deadly sin in Rwanda, especially for a man. 'He's gone to eat bread at Kilimadame's again,' she would murmur when she spotted a neighbour coming home from the market a little later than usual. For the women of Gitagata, 'eating bread at Kilimadame's' implied a betrayal far more serious than anything the little spectators sitting around the oven could imagine.

As you might expect, a loaf of bread bought from Nyira-bazungu, alias Kilimadame, became the ultimate reward for good schoolchildren. Reserved for the head of the class. The mothers took to selling whatever they could – bananas, beans, peanuts – and through countless priva-tions saving up a little fortune that they always kept on them, in the knot of their *pagne*, awaiting the day when they would spend it on the loaf of bread that had become the only acceptable prize for the top-ranked student. No mama doubted, and Stefania least of all, that for one of their children that day would come. Their only fear was that several might win that title at the same time, in which case they'd never have enough to buy them each the loaf they'd rightly earned.

The rankings were solemnly announced at the end of each trimester. The ceremony was held in the grounds of the school, the grounds where the trucks had abandoned the refugees a few years before, the school where Stefania had given birth to Julienne. But on the day of the results everyone tried to chase away those ugly memories and focus all their attention on the teachers awaiting the sign from the principal, their lists in their hands. The teachers stood in the middle of the schoolyard, the children made a circle around them, the anxious, intent parents pressed in behind, the mamas fingering the clutch of coins and a few rumpled bills knotted up in their *pagnes*, hoping they would soon undo that knot to reward the son or daughter they'd placed all their hopes in, the fathers leaning on the sticks they'd often used to threaten their progeny if their name wasn't one of the first three to be spoken.

The head of the class beamed with pride, less perhaps because of the excellence of his grades than because he'd earned the privilege of buying a loaf of bread in Kilimadame's shop with the coins entrusted to him by his emotional, trembling mother. A swarm of children followed him, shouting. He sat down before the front door of his house, for all to see. Or else he chose some strategic spot, preferably a termite mound, where everyone could watch him, admire him, and particularly admire the little loaf he held in his hand for a long time before he dared take a taste. He ate it down crumb by crumb. But more than the doughy, bland bread itself, it was his schoolmates' admiration, heavily tinged with envy, that he most wanted to savour for as long as he possibly could.

I too earned a loaf of Kilimadame's bread. Once, just once. It was in my fourth year of primary school, when Rose was my teacher. No sooner had she spoken my name than I raced toward Mama, who wept with joy as she smoothed the wadded bills she'd been keeping in the knot of her *pagne*, and I literally flew over the little eucalyptus woods that separated the schoolyard from the market square where Kilimadame had her shop. But once I held in my hand that bread I'd so longed for, I found I couldn't eat it all alone, like a glutton; I tore off half for my mother and shared the other half with Jeanne and Julienne. My friend Candida, who for all her tireless work had never managed to earn the supreme reward, also got a little piece for herself.

Even in Kigali, among the evolved people, bread remained a very special thing. Students at the Notre-Dame-de-Cîteaux high school didn't get bread; instead, at breakfast, there was a maggot-riddled porridge. We only got bread once a year, on Saint Nicholas's day. Ah! Saint Nicholas's day! We looked forward to that day from the very start of the year. The boldest students asked the Sisters if Saint Nicholas's day would be coming soon. Who this Saint Nicholas might be we had no idea: for us, Saint Nicholas's was the day we got bread. And what bread! A brioche shaped like a little man was awaiting each one of us at our place in the refectory. My persecutor, the head of our group, couldn't divide up the portions, and so that day, for once, I could be sure I'd get my share, exactly like everyone else's. Saint Nicholas's day! Some claimed to be sick a week before, since the ailing were given a larger share, and they could enjoy their little brioche man all alone in the tranquillity of their infirmary bed. And all through the week before the big day, an aroma so delicious it kept us awake streamed from Sister Marthe's kitchen. Sister Marthe herself seemed to have taken on the golden tint of the brioches she was baking, as if her cheeks had been impregnated with the abundance of oil and butter flowing through her kitchen that Saint Nicholas's Eve, like the land of Canaan's milk and honey whose wonders were vaunted by the Fathers, the nuns, and Papa's Bible. My one regret was that I couldn't bring a little piece of the Saint Nicholas man back to Mama and my sisters. The feast day was too far away from the nearest holiday for the brioche to last. All I could do was regale my little sisters with tales of Saint Nicholas's day's delights.

Imagine my surprise, on entering the School of Social Work in Butare, to find that the students got bread with their breakfast. So there was such a thing as the daily bread we prayed God to give us! So the Fathers hadn't been lying! How I regret having so soon been driven from that school in Butare, the only haven of freedom I knew in my youth! Never again do I want to see the image of my Hutu friends, boys from the public school, coming after me to kill me, me and my Tutsi schoolmates . . . But I've already written about that . . . I spent the week before the holiday conscientiously saving up my shares of bread so I could take them home to Stefania. On the day of our return to Nyamata, I had six loaves to put in my suitcase. I laid them in at the very bottom, under my pleated blue skirt and pink dress. It was Candida who gave me that dress, which she herself got from her big sister after much begging and blackmail. The pleated blue skirt I'd bought at the second-hand clothes stall in Kigali, with the money I'd made from my banana trees. Mama assigned each of her children a little garden plot, and the earnings from the harvest were our pocket money. That blue pleated skirt was like a dream. I'd seen one exactly like it on the Minister of Women's Affairs when she came to visit Notre-Dame-de-Cîteaux. She'd graduated from the School of Social Work, and one day I would study there myself, maybe I'd become a minister, so I needed a minister's skirt! That skirt cost me fifteen Rwandan francs, I think – probably less than a euro.

I almost forgot: there was also a t-shirt with a drawing of a big-eared mouse. Only much later did someone tell me his name was Mickey. I'm not sure it was meant to be worn with the minister's skirt. I couldn't wait to get home and give Mama those six loaves of bread.

I never saw Stefania eat one of my loaves of bread. She took them from me like precious treasures, as carefully and reverently as the priest picked up the blessed host, and stored them away in the little suitcase her oldest daughter Judith had brought back to her from the capital along with a white nylon t-shirt like the one only the schoolteacher Patricia could afford. Glowing with joy, she told me, 'This will be for the children.'

And the children of Gitagata heard Stefania had bread . . . They would come first thing in the morning. And Mama told them: 'Come, children, come and sit down next to me.' She ran to her little suitcase and took out a loaf, often white with mould. 'It's Moses's beard!' the children who went to catechism would laugh. Stefania brushed away the beard and handed around the bread. The white was streaked with dull green, which did nothing to spoil the children's excitement and gratitude. 'Now,' said Stefania, 'it's time for school. Promise me you'll work hard.' And sometimes the children came from far away, from Gitwe, from Cyohoha, from other villages, and they said, 'Stefania, I got the top grade!' And Stefania would run to her little suitcase, where there was always another piece of mouldy bread waiting.

At night, outside in the yard, my sisters and I looked up at the firmament. The firmament: that was a word we'd learnt from the Fathers. I liked that word. I said it to myself again and again. For us, the firmament was the little flock of clouds floating around the moon, like gilded flakes. And those clouds of the firmament could only be the marvellous loaves of bread that were waiting for us in heaven, the heaven over our heads or the one the Fathers were forever telling us about. But in any case, we were sure that in heaven there was much more bread, and much better bread, and much cheaper, than at Kilimadame's.

BEAUTY AND MARRIAGE

God's third commandment forbade all work on Sundays. He only meant the afternoon, since the morning was devoted to Mass. Going to the field or doing any big chore in the house meant gravely offending the Lord, we'd learnt, and should we disobey his commandment we might well see him appear astride storm clouds, red with anger, surrounded by tongues of flame like in the pictures the Fathers showed us at Mass. Some found that threat a little hard to swallow, but we were all thoroughly convinced that nothing could escape God's eye. We'd seen his eye in church, an eye that was always open. God was nothing but an eye. A sort of universal watchman who worked for no mayor or governor. And to make sure we believed it, they made us repeat in chorus, every Wednesday at catechism,

'*Mungu aba hose, abona byose, yumva byose, kandi azi byose* – God is everywhere, he sees all, he hears all, he knows all.'

And so the people of Gitagata had to somehow fill up a long, empty afternoon. The men went from house to house in search of a jug of sorghum beer. They stopped at the entrance to every enclosure and delivered an elaborate greeting to the people inside. If the mistress of the house had made beer, they were invited in to share. It was dark by the time they got home.

The women went out visiting too, but for them Sunday afternoon was above all a time for beauty treatments. Alas! No one in Gitagata had the miracle ointment that makes babies' limbs supple, that makes children's and young ladies' skin smooth and glistening, that holds the women's high hairdos in place, that preserves men's youthful glow: *ikimuri* – cow's milk butter. We had no cows in Gitagata, and no way to buy a dab of that beauty cream from the Bageseras, who themselves had so few. For the village mothers, the lack of *ikimuri* was one of the most painful reminders of exile. What would become of their children without that balm of eternal youth to give strength and beauty to their limbs? Later, when we managed to earn a little money from selling coffee, we went to the market and bought tiny bottles of peanut oil, whose powers couldn't begin to compare to *ikimuri*'s. And so the mamas made do with simply massaging their babies and shaving their little boys' and girls' heads, leaving only one very round tuft over their brows.

Once those children were teenagers and finally had the right to grow out their hair, Sunday afternoons were devoted to delousing. The delousing sessions were held in the back courtyard, behind the house: so private an operation had to be hidden from outsiders, or at least from the men. As always, Mama's friends and neighbours came and joined in: from them we had nothing to hide. As I've said, the back courtyard is the women's place, home to the open-air kitchen, sheltered under a straw roof and protected from the wind by mud walls. There the women gather to talk and roast corn. Men aren't allowed. They have no reason to be there anyway.

And so my mother would take her place on the termite mound, in the shade of the big spreading coffee plant. Julienne, Jeanne, and I sat on the ground, just beneath her. I couldn't see them, but I could feel Mama's fingers burrowing into the dense brush of my hair. As I recall, there were most often no lice, but my mother's fingers stayed for a good while in my thick hair, which to me felt like a long, slow caress.

Delousing went on until evening, because Mama often paused to chat with a visitor or stir the eternally cooking beans or chase away the monkeys ever watching for a chance to lay waste to our field. We moved on from spot to spot as the sun made its way toward the horizon. When its rays drove us away from the termite mound, we sat on the ground against the sorghum basket, and toward sunset we gathered under a banana tree, near the rack we used for drying manioc.

If there was no delousing to do on a Sunday afternoon, the women of Gitagata – and even some from further away – inevitably came to consult with Stefania on the subject of young women looking for husbands. Mama was a highly respected matchmaker. Her opinions on those young ladies carried a great deal of weight in the decisions of mothers seeking wives for their sons. They sat down on the termite mound, beneath the tall coffee plant. Stefania told the potential mother-in-law all the qualities and flaws of the girl under consideration. Was she from a respectable family? Did her manners and her nature bespeak a good upbringing? Was she a hard worker, unafraid to pick up a hoe? Did she show the promise of successful childbearing? And of course her beauty was subjected to painstaking scrutiny: did she walk with the grace of a cow, as the songs say? Did her eyes have the incomparable charm of a heifer's? Did she sway her bottom from side to side with the requisite majesty? Could you hear the quiet rustle of her thighs rubbing together as she walked by? Did she have a delicate network of stretch marks running over her legs?

It was no small task, living up to the canons of Rwandan beauty! That was in fact the favourite topic of conversation as the evening wore on. One by one, they listed the girls of marriageable age in Gitwe, Gitagata, Cyohoha, carefully following the order of the Tripolo houses. They laid out the candidates' good and bad points, particularly the bad. In Kinyarwanda that's known as *kunegurana*, and it inspires a good deal of laughter. Impartial judge that she was, Stefania never failed to note the progress she'd seen some of them make. No one was ever definitively condemned: redemption was always possible.

Young women looking for a husband knew the influence my mother could exert on the marriage arrangements, so they all found some pretext to come to our back courtyard and display themselves to Stefania, hoping to earn her approval. Girls primped for a stroll past our coffee plant even more than they did for Mass. It was a veritable beauty contest, a fashion show. They discreetly kept an eye on my mother, hoping for a promising sign. Those who got the nod knew they'd have no difficulty finding a husband.

I played a role of my own in these marriage matters. The role of a double agent. As it happens, little girls serve as confidants for marriageable young women. When the women go off to wash, carefully hidden behind the banana grove, the little girls follow them to scrub their backs. Everyone feels perfectly at ease to chat, and very soon personal secrets are being exchanged. With varying degrees of subtlety, the young women would try to draw me out, to learn what sorts of things Stefania was saying about them. I did my best to answer as vaguely as I could. They also wanted to know if my godmother Angelina, the wife of the teacher in the big school, the most elegant woman in Nyamata, might be willing to lend them one of her *pagnes* for the wedding or the party. Meanwhile, since they were showing themselves to me as God made them, I took the opportunity to give them a good looking-over, and then I passed on to Mama the beauties and defects revealed to me in the privacy of those ablutions. Of course, most of those women knew all about my espionage. Some willingly played along; others, for some reason, on the pretext of an inflexible modesty, refused.

But how can you learn for yourself whether you're beautiful or not when you don't have a mirror? There were no mirrors in Gitagata, not even in the shop; at the big store in Nyamata they were all on the top shelf, behind the counter – impossible to gaze deep into them, even when the salesman turned away to greet a new customer. Your only mirror was other people: your mother's admiring glances or sighs of distress, your big sister's or schoolmates' observations and appraisals, and then the village chatter, which would inevitably end up finding its way to you: who's beautiful? who's not?

But how can you be sure, with no mirror, that at least some of your features meet the criteria of beauty vaunted by matchmakers and celebrated in songs, proverbs, and stories: lush hair, a high forehead, a straight nose (the little nose that meant death for so many Rwandans), black gums like Stefania's (a sign of good ancestry), gapped teeth . . .? When the sun shone just so, you could bend down over a puddle and try to glimpse your reflection. But that liquid portrait wiggled before your helpless eyes. Your watery face wavered, contracted, fragmented into little dots of light. Your face would never be yours, as it was when it was trapped in the mirror: it was always for others.

If you wanted to be elegant and refined, you had only to follow Mama's advice and example: imitate the village ladies' lazy, swaying walk (with every step they took they seemed to be standing in place), let a slightly vacant gaze drift over the people around you, and above all, when someone speaks to you, always keep your eyes lowered (how shameful it is for a young girl to look someone in the face!), answer in a fluting voice, all but inaudible, a soft murmur, a melodious whisper . . . For your hair too, you had to rely on others. There were no hairdressers, neither in Gitagata nor in Nyamata; as for the men, they went to the *kimyozi*, who had the only pair of scissors in the village – apart from Berkmasse the tailor, of course – and set out a chair for his customers beneath a big fig tree, beside the dirt road. So it was your sister or a schoolfriend who cut those regular, crescent-moon shaped tufts from the thick curls of your hair, those tufts we call *amasunzu*, worn by all girls before marriage. Visiting the gardens of grand old chateaux in France, I told myself that the kings had their boxwood hedges shaped just the way we shaped our hair. I didn't dare share that comparison with my erudite guide, who was telling me about a gardener by the name of Le Nôtre.

But *amasunzu* weren't for little girls, or even young adolescents. Your hairstyle depended on your age. The smallest children, girls and boys alike, had their heads shaved, leaving just one very round little tuft, like a pompom, above the forehead. With puberty, when they turned twelve or thirteen, their hair was allowed to grow. The girls never cut it. If it was long enough, they tied it back behind their heads. You didn't wear *amasunzu* until you were eighteen or even twenty years old. That meant you were old enough to marry, looking for a husband, waiting for your Prince Charming, as they'd say in France. At the same age, the girls gave up the little swath of fabric that served as their skirt, and draped themselves in the respectable *pagne* worn by married women and mothers. The *amasunzu* allowed people to tell the difference.

I never got to wear *amasunzu*. At my high school in Kigali I was too young, and in any case preoccupation with your appearance was considered worse than all the seven deadly sins put together. When we went out on Sundays, under the watchful eye of an escort of nuns, nothing was supposed to attract longing gazes from boys – or, worse yet, according to Sister Kizito, from married men. But who would ever have noticed us, with our respectably modest grey uniforms and close-cropped hair?

Things were very different at the School of Social Work in Butare. The new fashions of the city, introduced by a few particularly daring students, were liberally tolerated, if not encouraged, by most of the teachers. No more *amasunzu* – that was an archaic, degrading custom. Straight hair was the order of the day, and the new ideal for fashionable girls. But only a privileged few owned the tool required for the procedure: a metal comb with many close-set teeth and a wooden handle. All you had to do was heat it in the fire until it glowed, then run it through the untamed wilderness of your curls, and they would be transformed into long, silky locks that draped over your shoulders. What would we not have given to get our hands on that miracle comb! But it was virtually impossible to convince someone to lend it out. That instrument's lucky owners, the daughters of rich shopkeepers or high-ranking functionaries, were determined to keep it for themselves, and so maintain their monopoly on unkinked hair. But that proud monopoly didn't last long. We poor country folk soon found another way to straighten. We discovered it in the laundry room, where, on Saturday afternoons, we washed our clothes and pressed them with charcoal-heated irons. Those irons were heavy, and more unwieldy than the comb, but if you got them hot enough, they too could straighten hair. 'We're going to iron our hair,' we used to say, laughing. To make the operation still more effective, we rubbed our hair with lard we discreetly scraped from our morning toast, that delicious lard that was our butter! Needless to say, the results didn't always measure up to our expectations, and sometimes our hair looked more like porcupine quills than the long, flowing locks we were dreaming of. Still, the occasional mishap notwithstanding, our ironed locks could rival the rich girls' comb-straightened hair. In France, ten years later, I couldn't wait to get my hands on one of those miraculous combs I'd coveted for so long. 'Is that for a poodle?' the cashier asked me.

When the holiday came and I went home to Gitagata with my new hairdo, Mama voiced no objection. She touched my hair, went and sat down on the termite mound to look me over, and concluded that this was progress, *amajyambere*, just like in the motto of our Republic. But she was also convinced that the cool of the mountains in Rwanda had helped repair what the blazing sun of the Bugesera had burned onto my head.

Amajyambere, progress, development, the inevitable theme of our mayor's speeches, was mostly brought across the Nyabarongo by the few Nyamatan children who'd been admitted to secondary school. Wearing drawers, for instance: it was I myself who introduced that innovation to our household. Underwear was mandatory at the Notre-Dame-de-Cîteaux high school. The trousseau that students were required to assemble included two pairs of drawers – two *ikaliso*. Stefania and I went to consult with Berkmasse, the tailor. He knew what we meant. For a modest price, he cut my two pairs of drawers from spare scraps of cloth. I reverently laid them into the little cardboard suitcase that was Alexia's before it was mine.

Those two *ikaliso* were for the first trimester; for the second, we had to buy a piece of cloth, white cotton, known as *americani*. We brought it to sewing class, most of which was devoted to making drawers for ourselves. We were all supposed to have a full supply. The teacher, Madame Julia – a Belgian woman whose lips, to our great astonishment, were as red as the beak of the bird we call *ifundi* – terrorised us with the big stick she used for measuring fabric in yards and inches. We called her Kamujijima, a nickname whose meaning I've never completely understood, but which obviously had something to do with the fear she inspired in us. After a few weeks, all the new girls were wearing the same sort of drawers as the longtime students. They came down almost to our knees. Every evening, in the dormitory, our *ikaliso* were the focal point of a curious ritual: after the prayer, we were supposed to take them off before the inquisitive eye of the sister on duty, then shake them in cadence and very carefully drape them over the rail at the foot of the bed, for the nun's inspection. And we drifted off to sleep, with our drawers fluttering at the feet of our beds, like the banners of civilisation triumphant!

And indeed, the nuns were counting on us to spread the use of underwear into our villages. We'd been named evangelists for underwear. The *ikaliso*! That was one innovation that fascinated all the girls who'd stayed behind in the village. I sometimes caught one of my younger sisters opening my suitcase and discreetly taking out a pair of my *ikaliso*, which she must have promised to show one of her friends. But for a long time drawers were reserved for the few girls who, like me, had earned a place in secondary school. They were a point of pride for us intellectuals, a privilege for girls alone, because while the boys who went to seminary came home with a pair of khaki shorts that we called *ikabutura*, they wore nothing underneath them. The Fathers didn't concern themselves with such things. And besides, people said, what's the point of putting on a second *ikabutura* under the first?

Stefania approved of that intimate innovation the moment she saw it on me. She immediately asked me (in secret) to sew her a pair of drawers according to Kamujijima's pattern. They were her pride and joy. She told all her friends of the many advantages drawers gave a girl, but everyone guessed it was her own drawers she was vaunting.

Nonetheless, for Mama, the principal force for development was not me, or Alexia, or even André. It was our neighbour Marie-Thérèse, Pancrace's wife. She criticised her, of course, on the grounds that Marie-Thérèse was often too quick to adopt the new ways, but she always kept an eye on her, and sometimes she ended up imitating her. Everyone knew who was behind the novelties we first saw only at Pancrace's house: Félicité, Marie-Thérèse's oldest daughter, who was at the convent school run by the Benebikira Sisters, I've forgotten where, maybe in Save. In the Rwanda of the Belgians or President Kayibanda, joining the church was the surest, smoothest path to 'civilisation'. In seminaries and convent schools, the clothes, the food, the bedding, everything – or almost – was just like the white people's. If you were properly fervent in your obedience to the rules of conduct and piety that were imposed on you, then without too much effort you could enter the much-envied ranks of the evolved people. And so, thanks to Félicité, her family enjoyed all modernity's latest advances, which, despite some sneering and jealousy, spread inexorably from house to house.

Félicité! She scandalised more than one Gitagatan when she convinced her father to build a little house just for her next to the Tripolo house. Who ever heard of such a thing? A girl who wasn't married – who, if she went on following the weird ideas of the white people, might never marry at all – living alone, sleeping alone, without her sisters, yes without her sisters! People found it shocking, an affront to all our traditions, wanting to sleep all alone when she had so many little sisters who naturally had a place beside her on the mat. The whole village talked of nothing but Félicité's 'home', a word she'd brought back from the convent school, a word unknown to the big kids in the sixth year of primary school, and even to their teacher, a word that to our ears shrouded the much-decried dwelling in deep mystery. It's true that Félicité never opened her door to anyone in the village, not even the neighbours. Nevertheless, Candida and I came up with all sorts of pretexts to be invited inside. It never worked. Félicité told us in great detail of the extraordinary life she lived with the Benebikira Sisters, but only outside the front door of her 'home', which remained adamantly closed.

Still, there were whispers that that door might not be forbidden to everyone. Why, people wondered, had the little house been built not behind the Tripolo house, in the *ikigo*, the area set aside for women, but next to the road, near the coffee plants? So she could receive visits from boys, obviously. And all day long, even deep into the night, we heard music coming from that 'home': Félicité played the *inanga*, the eight-stringed zither, which is strictly prohibited for women. And often she strolled along the dirt road with her *inanga*, which, we soon realised, was not our traditional *inanga* but the white people's, a guitar, and she sang and the children followed her and repeated in chorus the canticles she'd learnt from the nuns. Everyone was firmly convinced of it: that was progress, *amajyambere*, parading for better or worse down Gitagata's dirt road.

But there was more – another little house, I mean, smaller, more or less adjoining the first. We couldn't quite figure out what its purpose might be. It was too small to lay out a mat in, too small to cook in, and it clearly wasn't meant for drying manioc or storing sorghum. Like the door of the 'home', its door was always closed. Stefania discreetly kept an eye on that tiny house, and one day the door happened to be open, revealing Félicité comfortably seated, her skirt hitched up, on a sort of wooden bench. There was no room for doubt: that little house was a latrine, Félicité's latrine.

When that revelation spread through Gitagata, it caused a great deal of reflection. For most of us, the latrines were a big ditch at the far end of the banana grove. We did our business together. Sometimes, at night, a soldier on patrol fell in. We could hear his cries. That made us laugh and laugh, but we still feared his vengeance. The more refined among us covered the ditch with big logs, leaving only a little square hole that you squatted over. There were even some, like us, who surrounded it with a wall of branches, but there was never any sort of roof. We couldn't imagine relieving ourselves without the sun and the clouds over our heads. At night, if you had to get up, there was no question of going all the way to the latrine. Crossing through the banana grove meant risking an unpleasant encounter: a snake, a leopard, a soldier. We went no further than the *ikigo*, but the next morning everyone was supposed to clear away anything they'd left there, down to the tiniest trace. You had to recognise your own excrement, which often caused long, drawn-out arguments, always settled by Stefania, who assured us that as a mother she could unfailingly tell what was whose.

Little by little, thanks to Marie-Thérèse, whose daughter eventually allowed her to use the little house, we were given a very faithful description of what Félicité, still according to her mother, called her WC. What's truly amazing, Marie-Thérèse told us, is that you sit on a piece of pottery shaped like your bottom, you could stay there for hours! We had some trouble understanding that the piece of pottery in question was the neck of a jug that had been carefully decapitated and served as a toilet bowl, like the ones I discovered much later in Butare. For that matter, Marie-Thérèse added, you could have the Batwa potters make you one ... The fashion of the new WCs introduced by Félicité quickly spread in Gitagata. Women talked their husbands into digging new trenches so they could install the same facilities as Marie-Thérèse. It was progress, *amajyambere*! How could they have known that many of them were digging their own graves?

Among all the new things Marie-Thérèse displayed for her neighbours' envy with what must have been a slightly wicked delight, there was one that Stefania immediately embraced with enthusiasm. Marie-Thérèse had a lot of white hair. White hair was not admired on a woman, unless she was a respectable grandmother. She tried to hide it under a scarf, but often a stray lock would give her away. For all her efforts, the whole village knew Marie-Thérèse had white hair. But one day we saw her come out of her house with no scarf, and every eye was riveted to her hair: it was intensely black, and it glistened. Far blacker than our skin, some of that black had even dripped down her forehead, leaving long, dark trails behind it. Marie-Thérèse refused to explain her hair's metamorphosis. Mama didn't dare question her any further, but she was determined to uncover her secret.

It was Félicité's little sister Assumpta who gave the secret away. Assumpta was a regular Sunday-afternoon visitor in our back courtyard. Like all the other would-be brides, she paraded her charms before the jury that held court on the termite mound, presided over by Stefania, who soon wormed the truth out of her. Assumpta very proudly explained that Félicité had brought home a black powder some of the ageing nuns used to dye their hair. Like all mysterious drugs, it was said to have come from Zanzibar. As it happened, you could get hold of it at the market in Kigali. It went by the name of Kanta. At the end of the holiday, on the day I was to head back to Kigali, Mama discreetly slipped into my bindle a few coins she'd set aside from her hard work and buried under the bed, whispering in my ear, 'Don't forget to bring me some of that hair powder.'

And then there were our feet! So many worries our feet gave us! If, still according to the Rwandan standard of beauty, very straight legs were prized, with no ugly bulge at the calf, the feet were supposed to be small and delicate, with long, slender toes. But how could you keep your feet comely when you had to walk barefoot on the dirt road, and till the soil from morning to evening, still barefoot? At the school in Kigali, the city girls found it easy to mock us country folk, our feet incrusted with indelible dirt. If they wanted to know who you were, where you came from, the first thing people did was look at your feet. Not even the teachers were spared. At the School of Social Work in Butare, the moment a new girl came through the front gate, the veterans warned her: 'Whatever you do, don't look at Upper Volta's feet!' That sentence, which the older girls repeated again and again with a knowing air, plunged my friends and me into deep perplexity. How were we to interpret it? Was it wise counsel, was it a riddle, was it a code we were meant to decipher, a trap laid for us first-year innocents by our elders? Come what may, we were all bent on uncovering the mystery of Upper Volta's feet. The afternoon of the first day, in the big assembly hall, the principal, surrounded by every last member of the teaching staff, presented the establishment to us. Most of the teachers were nuns. They were all white but one. The black woman had to be Upper Volta. All the new girls immediately lowered their eyes to Upper Volta's feet, but no: her dress came down all the way to the floor, completely covering her feet. So there really was some mystery about Upper Volta's feet, since we'd all noticed the other nuns' dresses weren't as long, and you could see their feet and the little sandals they wore. Upper Volta alone hid her feet. What deformity, what hideousness did she have to conceal beneath the drapery of her dress? A few days later, the secret of Upper Volta's feet was revealed in all its horror. We were in class when Upper Volta came in to make some sort of announcement. The teacher's desk sat on a low platform, two steps up from the floor. If Upper Volta climbed onto the platform, she'd have to lift up the hem of her dress to keep from stumbling, and her feet would inevitably be revealed. Every eye was fixed on that hem. What would she do? She seemed to hesitate. Had she noticed the strange vigilance aimed her way? Finally she made up her mind, boldly clutched the fabric of her dress, and, as quickly as she could without abandoning her teacherly dignity, she scaled the two wooden steps. Not quickly enough, though, because we'd had time – a low murmur ran through the classroom – yes, we'd had time to see, to see Upper Volta's feet.

I won't try to describe Upper Volta's feet, but I remember that, some time later, paging through our history and geography textbook, I discovered two drawings or photographs, I'm no longer sure which, that immediately reminded me of Upper Volta's feet. One showed mountains or hills that had been cut away like a slice of cake, exposing the superimposed layers of earth and stone thanks to which, as we were taught, geologists could decipher the history of the continents and number the eras of the earth. The second showed a sort of trench dug by archaeologists, who, said the caption, had thereby uncovered, from a handful of faintly chipped stones in the deepest strata, the first known traces of mankind. And it seemed to me that had I got a good look at Upper Volta's feet, I too might have been able to read the eras of the earth and work my way back from generation to generation until I reached the woman who, with her back bent and a hoe in her hand, first broke the red soil of Africa. But I was young, and that thought frightened me. I looked at my feet and the high-heeled shoes given to me in Kigali by my friend Immaculée. Deeply relieved, I assured myself that my feet could still slip into them. But today I might well kiss Upper Volta's feet, and most certainly Mama's, and the feet of all those women who'd served as foster mothers to Africa.

ANTOINE'S WEDDING

My mother's widely acknowledged gift for arranging marriages nevertheless met with one failure – and what a failure, since it involved the marriage of her oldest son Antoine! Mama had searched and searched for a fiancée for Antoine, but she had to be perfect, and no girl of Gitagata or anywhere else could come close to that ideal. Then, one fine day, a new family came and settled a little outside Gitagata, toward Lake Cyohoha. I don't recall where they came from, maybe Kanzenze, off in the valley of the Nyabarongo, or even further away, from Bwanacyambwe, not far from Kigali. Everyone in Gitagata looked down their noses at the newcomers: the universal opinion was that they were very lowly people, the proof being that they had only three children, and worse yet three girls! Furthermore, rumour had it they were pagans, because the three girls didn't even have Christian names. And it's true, we only knew them by their Rwandan names: Mukantwari, Mukarukinga, and Mukasine.

All this gossip and disparagement didn't stop my mother from setting her eye on one of the three sisters, the oldest, Mukasine. She immediately recognised her as the future wife she'd so long been seeking for Antoine. It was a gift from heaven, it was a miracle! She offered thanks to the Virgin Mary, along with Ryangombe, the Master of the Spirits. My mother was a good Christian, but she said you shouldn't leave anyone out, especially not the gods of our ancestors. 'You have to weed all the sorghum plants,' she liked to say. 'You never know which will be the first to bear fruit.' Mary or Ryangombe, she didn't know which, had answered her prayers, so it was best to keep them both on her side.

In my mother's eyes, Mukasine was beauty personified: very tall (she got that from her father, who was like a spear), light-skinned (the colour we call *inzobe*, not to be confused with the kind of unsightly paleness that supposedly attracts lightning bolts), full hair (like Mukasonga's, she raved), a shapely rump, and those legs! and those thighs! Mukasine had all the graces Rwandans attribute to the cow, but she had them in their most perfect form: she was an *inyambo*, a royal cow! And indeed, wasn't her name

Isine, the cow with the lustrous bronze coat? My mother said it again and again: she'd found an *inyambo*!

Obviously, physical beauty wasn't the only quality required for a potential bride. In the misery and poverty of our Nyamatan exile a good wife was expected to know how to work. To her would fall the task of cultivating the field to keep the family fed: ploughing the earth, weeding, barefoot in the mud, hands covered with calluses from the hoe. A good mother never shirked, no matter how arduous the task. My mother intended to make sure Mukasine was as hard-working as she was beautiful, and so several times she got up well before dawn and walked the two kilometres to Mukasine's house. On the pretext of visiting friends in the neighbourhood, she spent all day long spying on the woman who would perhaps soon be her daughter-in-law. She came back greatly pleased with the results of her espionage. Mukasine got up early, and she was as beautiful first thing in the morning as she was in the bright noontime sun. But above all she was a tireless worker, she never took a moment's rest, she veritably ripped up the fields, in the words of my jubilant mother.

Stefania didn't try to hide that this ardour for work was the source of one physical flaw, the only one she'd detected in Mukasine. The beautiful Mukasine had enormous feet, real peasant feet, creased, slashed, cracked, lumpy with corns. With every step, she looked as if she was picking up two huge clods of dirt. 'Oh well!' said

Mama. 'Better those than some princess's feet that have never once touched the ground!'

There was no reason to hesitate any longer: Mukasine was the wife Antoine needed, the one Mama had so long been waiting for. Now the various steps necessary for a proposal had to be undertaken as quickly as possible, because even if she'd told no one of her intentions, she feared such a prize might well catch the eye of many others.

And so one evening, after we ate, close by the three stones of the hearth where my little sisters and I gathered to hear her stories, Mama told my father of her plans for Antoine. She listed Mukasine's many qualities, and concluded that they mustn't wait to officially ask for her hand. My father could only approve. The one person who wasn't there to offer his opinion was Antoine. He worked in Karama all week long, and came home only on Saturday night before going off again on Sunday afternoon. I fear my mother hadn't bothered to let him in on her plans.

In Rwandan tradition, many steps must be taken to seal a marriage contract. My father's first task was to pay a call on Mukasine's parents and announce his intention of asking for their daughter's hand on his son's behalf. Evidently everything went smoothly, but still my father didn't come home from that first mission until evening – not because the negotiations had proved difficult, but no doubt because the accord had been celebrated with several calabashes of beer.

Next we had to solemnly make the formal request. That required long preparations. Appearing before the future fiancée's parents without the jugs of beer the ceremony demanded was out of the question, so the whole family got to work. Since our banana trees were too young to bear enough fruit, and despite the good will of the neighbours who contributed what they could, we had to go and buy bananas from the Bageseras. My job, as soon as I came home from school, after I'd gone to fetch water, was to take my place at the millstone and crush sorghum. I never left the *urusyo*, I had to grind, grind, grind . . . The girls of the neighbourhood took turns helping out, and one by one the baskets were lined up on the *uruhimbi*. We knew we'd be needing lots of beer, because the girl's parents always invite the whole family to hear the proposal, every last one of them, and all their friends, and their friends' friends, and even people who aren't really friends at all, not to mention the passing strangers who absolutely must be allowed to dip their straw in the jug.

On the day, my father, followed by a long, jug-bearing cortege – almost all the young men of Gitagata – left to formally propose the marriage. He was accompanied by his best friend Édouard, because the proposal speech must be delivered not by the father but by a worthy known for his eloquence. Édouard, who like my father was often called on to resolve local conflicts, was just the man for the job. Antoine had finally been told of the plans being laid for him, but he was not part of the delegation; his job was to stay home with his friends and wait for news, making a great show of his nervousness. To be sure, the outcome was never in doubt. The orators on both sides exchanged speeches. They made it very clear it was Mukasine whose hand they were asking for, not Mukantwari or Mukarukinga. And then, the proposal having been accepted, the assembled crowd could justly celebrate the event over the jugs of beer we'd worked so hard to brew.

But don't think that's all there is to it. The proposal isn't fully valid until it's confirmed, and so the same ceremony must be performed three full times. It's a long process; before each one you have to make up the jugs of beer everyone is expecting. At the third ceremony, the promise of marriage is made official by the delivery of the dowry to the girl's family. Alas, in Antoine's case, the process that seemed to have begun so auspiciously was abruptly interrupted by an event as unexpected as it was scandalous: the abduction of the beautiful Mukasine.

A certain Kabugu lived across from the lot where Mukasine's family had settled. That noble personage – he was a member of the royal clan – had shielded himself from want by marrying one of his daughters to a white man. Thanks to that marriage, he could hire other refugees to cultivate his field – the newcomers still waiting for their first harvest, always looking for odd jobs to tide themselves over. That must have been how Mukasine went to work for her well-to-do neighbour, and how her beauty and industriousness caught the eye of Kabugu's wife, who was looking for a mate for her son. That son was a longtime bachelor: people said he would never find a wife. And now here was just the wife they'd been looking for, coming to call, so to speak, right in the suitor's enclosure! The opportunity was too good to pass up. What did it matter that others had got a head start in their plans and asked for Mukasine's hand according to all the rules and conventions? Kabugu and his wife cared nothing about the conventions: they needed Mukasine, and so they would take her.

The entire village was shocked and horrified by the news of Mukasine's disappearance. Everyone condemned Kabugu's act and sympathised with my distraught family. But the damage was done. There was no point in dwelling on it. Mukasine had been abducted after dark. Willingly or by force, she'd spent the night in the son's house. She couldn't go back to her parents; nor of course could she become Antoine's wife. There were even those who insinuated that Mukasine's parents weren't entirely unhappy to see their daughter marrying the son of rich Kabugu. So who knows, maybe they didn't really object to the abduction ... People advised my father to demand they return the gifts he'd brought to pave the way for the marriage. But my father had his pride, and my mother firmly stated that taking back gifts given in Antoine's name would bring us misfortune. All we had left was the cow meant to serve as the dowry.

When I think back on that sad story, I find myself wondering if that cow itself might have been partly responsible for Mukasine's abduction: it took us so long to get hold of it! In Rwanda, the gift of a cow is required to seal a marriage pact. But the people of Nyamata had no cows. In 1959, the Hutus had burned their enclosures, and the cows too had burned in their stables. And so, with some shame and much sadness, the refugees resigned themselves to settling a marriage with nothing more than a basket of beans or sorghum and a few banknotes saved up with great difficulty.

But to my mother, Antoine's marriage could only be properly celebrated with the gift of a cow: a dowry that failed to respect the traditions would bring the couple bad luck, she thought. Our only choice was to scrape together enough money to buy a cow. That took a long time, and it forced us into many privations. The meagre salary Antoine earned in Karama obviously wasn't enough, so we had to sell whatever we could: bananas, beans, sorghum. We ate only the bad beans, carefully sorted out by Mama. I went to the Nyamata market to sell peanuts or wild tomatoes that I gathered on the banks of Lake Cyohoha. My parents even skimmed a little from Alexia and André's tuition money. Food, clothes, school: everything was sacrificed for that cow.

Meanwhile, my father spent his days in Gahanga, beyond the Nyabarongo, just outside Kigali, at the live-stock market. He inspected the animals, he enquired into their price, he bargained. He had to find a cow whose beauty would be worthy of Mukasine's, a cow that could also be called *Isine*, the cow with the lustrous bronze coat.

One night, we were awakened by a great commotion: it was my father and Antoine, bringing home the glorious cow. Since there were no little boys in the household, it fell to me to look after her as we waited for the big day, when, with all the solemnity the occasion required, she would be given to the future in-laws. We know how that turned out.

Mama never lost heart. She had a son to marry, and a cow for the dowry. She set off again in search of a fiancée for Antoine. She devoted her days and nights to the task. Finally she was told of a girl named Jeanne who might fit the bill. She was younger than Mukasine and every bit as beautiful, with a lineage my mother approved of. She lived far away, in Cyugaro, a full twenty kilometres distant. That didn't stop my mother from going off to verify first-hand the accuracy of the information she'd been given. She came home more or less satisfied, but to confirm her first impression she sent Alexia and me to ask, on what pretext I don't know, for hospitality from the presumptive fiancée's family, who gladly took us in, proud to have under their roof an intellectual like Alexia, who was in secondary school. On our return home, we made a favourable report; Jeanne and Alexia were more or less the same age, and they'd become fast friends. And so the cow was given as dowry to Jeanne's family, and she became Antoine's wife. They had nine children, seven of them boys, to my mother's delight. She was sure at least a few of them would survive to carry on the family name. She was wrong.

THE LAND OF STORIES

The time has come to blow out the flickering little flame of the *agatadowa*. We've finished eating. Dinner didn't take long, first because there wasn't much to eat, but also because, for a Rwandan, eating is always just a bit shameful. We don't like opening our mouths in front of other people. Papa has already long since cleaned his plate. He doesn't eat with us in the common room. A father doesn't eat in front of his children. He has his own little vestibule, in front of the door to the courtyard. He eats behind the mat that serves as a curtain, on the low seat reserved only for men. The youngest child, Jeanne, goes to take away his plate. Papa has left her a few beans and sweet potatoes: a father must always set something aside for his youngest child. Now there's nothing more to do in the Tripolo house. It's not a restful feeling. Fear is always lurking. Mama blows out the oil lamp made from a tin can Antoine bought from Haguma, a houseboy to white people in Karama. Hurry, let's get back to the *inzu*!

Mama puts a little fresh wood on the fire burning in the middle of the basin. Revived, the flame fills the vault of the *inzu* with a warm, amber light. Mama sits down on her mat against the screen that shelters the big bed. She stretches out her legs. She unties the piece of cloth she uses as a scarf, salvaged from her old *pagne*. She carefully folds it and lays it on the rim of a basket of beans. We three girls are all sitting facing her. Little by little the heat from the nearby fire works its way into us, filling us with a blissful torpor, now the fire is just a peaceful red glow. The storytelling hour has come . . .

Mama always begins with a sad song, a song sung by cowherd girls, the kind she used to sing when she was little, as she tended the herd by the banks of the Rukarara. Often it was the story of a poor little cowherd who lost his cows. They escaped, they crossed the river, now they're grazing on foreign grass. The cowherd set off to look for them in a canoe, but, I don't know why, the song says the river will swallow him up, along with his herd:

Yewe musare wari
ku muvumba

wambutsa ubwato
n'ingashya
Rwankubito araje . . .

I didn't listen to my mother's stories (told only at night, because if they were told during the day a person might turn into a lazy lizard that spends its whole life basking in the sun), I didn't listen to Stefania's stories, but in the half-sleep I sank into, lulled by her tireless murmur and the hypnotic heat of the hearth, the sound of them penetrated my half-numb body, impregnated the slow drift of my reveries . . . And sometimes today my drowsy thoughts open up that land of stories to me again.

No, I'm not a stranger to the land of stories. I know what those chattering gourds have to say to the eleusine plant. I know why the toad croaks and pridefully puffs himself up: with the help of all his brothers, he beat the wagtail in a race. I know what lets out that piteous wail in the savannah: it's the *impereryi*, the little animal Imana forgot to give a tail. It pushes and pushes all night long, trying to squeeze out the beautiful appendage it was denied. It's a bad idea to listen to its mournful plaint for too long, and an even worse idea to twist your head around to try to see your own backside. I know why that man leaves his enclosure every night. He's headed for the forest. And this evening he's carrying a little basket. And in that little basket there's a woman's breast, the breast he tore off his wife, which he's promised his lover, the girl of the forest, who has only one. But long before dawn, the sage has pulled his spear from the ground (for what would a man be without his spear?); all day long, he'll walk the path along the hilltops, and when night falls, in the enclosure, before a packed crowd of elders, he will consult the white-haired child. And the little cowherd can ask me his question: 'Is there such a thing as shared love?' I know the answer: 'Little cowherd, your master loves only his sterile wife, who only has eyes for her cousin, who went off to join the king of Cyamakombe, whom he admires more than anyone alive, but the king of Cyamakombe cares only for his daughter, who's fallen deeply in love with a ram with an immaculate fleece . . .' And you, do you know why the insatiable Sebugugu weeps? He followed the blackbird's advice and killed his only cow. 'Sacrifice your cow,' the blackbird had chirped to him, 'and you'll get a hundred more.' Also, beware of girls who are too beautiful; some of them are lionesses in disguise. The sight of raw meat will reveal their true savage nature. Now, I'm not going to tell you what you might find in the stomach of the hyena, but I will tell the king where to find the girl he's meant to marry: she's in the butter churn, that poor orphan girl, held captive by her stepmother's wicked spells . . .

I don't want to venture into the furthest reaches of the land of stories, because I know what's waiting for me. Beside the vast swamps, there's a hunched little old woman. She hides her face beneath her ragged *pagne*, but I know she's staring at me with eyes that have no light left in them.

She's the one who agreed to house Death in her sterile belly.

But there were other stories. Stories that weren't ours, stories we didn't tell around the fire. Stories that were like the toxic drugs concocted by poisoners, stories heavy with hatred, heavy with death. The stories told by the white people, the Bazungu.

The Bazungu had unleashed all the insatiable monsters of nightmares on the Tutsis. They held up the distorting mirrors of their untruths, and in the name of their science and their religion, we were made to see ourselves in the malevolent double their fantasies had given birth to.

The Bazungu claimed to know better than us who we were, where we came from. They'd examined us, they'd weighed us, they'd measured us. Their conclusions were final: our skulls were Caucasian, our profiles Semitic, our figures Nilotic. They even knew the name of our progenitor: it was in the Bible, his name was Ham. We were virtually white (despite some regrettable crossbreeding): a little bit Jewish, a little bit Aryan. The experts, and for this we were meant to be grateful, had even concocted a tailor-made race just for us: we were Hamites!

Those same experts had uncovered the Tutsis' traces all over the world: they'd driven their massive herds down from the high plateaus of Tibet, they didn't stay long on the plains of the Ganges or the Indus, they briefly joined up with the Exodus of the Hebrews, mixing with them a bit in the confusion of the campgrounds. They fraternised with the entourage of the pharaohs, then ended up in Ethiopia, the Ethiopia of Prester John, where they just barely missed becoming Christians. Finally (and in this no doubt Providence had a hand), they came to Rwanda, to the mountains of the moon, they were made guardians of the sources of the Nile, waiting for the baptismal water to moisten the brow of some Hamite Constantine.

Businiya! I don't know how that hateful story reached my mother's ears. She knew, of course, like all Rwandans, that in the beginning Kigwa fell from the sky with all the domesticated animals and cultivated plants, that Gihanga organised human society by dividing the tasks between his three sons, each according to his talents: Gatutsi would milk the cows, Gahutu would milk the earth, and Gatwa would milk the forest. But she also knew about Businiya. She told me about it while we were out weeding the sorghum: 'You know, some people say the Tutsis came from Businiya.' She recounted the story of a strange exodus: the Tutsis had walked and walked, from hill to hill, their belongings in little bundles on their heads. She believed that long walk took place in Kenya, where the Tutsis had to fight with the fierce giants that lived in that land. Strangely, according to my mother, that migration happened exactly when the white people came.

Businiya! Abyssinia! Where had my mother picked up that story, when for her the universe ended at the borders of Rwanda? Orphaned, she'd been taken in by the nuns at Kansi who put her to work cooking, cleaning, and sewing. Was that where she'd heard and remembered that strange word Abyssinia, which she'd turned into Businiya? Was it an echo of the conversations of the evolved people in the circle of sub-chief Ruvebana, whom my father served as secretary and confidant? Wanting to make it a good story, she filled it out with bits of the Good Book she'd gleaned more or less accurately from the Sunday sermons or the Bible readings the head of our family gave us each evening. Businiya, Abyssinia, Ethiopia: how could my mother have foreseen that those words would bring death to so many of us?

One year, I don't remember when, I came home from school for the long holiday and proudly announced to my mother: 'Mama! I saw the king of Businiya.' Stefania stared at me in silence, surprised and incredulous, then took her head in her hands and began to moan: 'My daughter Mukasonga doesn't know what she's saying any more. Do you hear her, Holy Virgin, and you, Ryangombe, god of our fathers, she says she saw the king of Businiya! Can anyone see the king of Businiya? The king of Businiya! She says she saw the king of Businiya!' But I refused to back down: 'It's true, I saw him, he came to Kigali.'

I wasn't lying. Haile Selassie, the King of Kings, the emperor of Ethiopia, had indeed come to Rwanda on an official visit. No efforts were spared in Kigali to give the oldest and greatest African head of state a lavish welcome. The road from the airport was lined with triumphal arches of greenery, and banners welcoming the illustrious guest in several languages. The streets were adorned with banana trees, and the eucalyptus trunks were painted white up to regulation height. The Lycée Notre-Dame-de-Cîteaux participated in this to-do. We'd been given new uniforms of a cut we found daring, much to our delight. They'd handed out little flags with the two countries' colours, and we practised waving them all together, in unison.

The announcement that the king of Businiya would be visiting had filled me with deep excitement. I was going to see the king of that storied land where my mother said the Tutsis had come from! I didn't dare imagine what he'd look like, but I was sure he'd be very tall, almost a giant, with a gown even grander than the one Monsignor wears for confirmation, and on his head I pictured a crown as tall as the papal tiara.

How long we waited for that emperor of Ethiopia! The girls from Notre-Dame-de-Cîteaux had been very visibly placed at the main roundabout in the city, in front of the Sainte-Famille church. Braving the disdainful stares of my Hutu schoolmates, I'd worked my way to the front row. It was a hot day. Our arms were all aching from waving our little flags. We jumped every time a car came along. No, still not him!

Finally the official motorcade turned onto the airport road. First we saw the military trucks, then the ministers' black Mercedes, and then at long last I spotted, standing in a roofless car – some sort of jeep, I suppose – the man I was so eagerly awaiting. I stared at him intently, as if the force of my gaze might stop his car for a few moments, just for me, but it was already speeding away. It must be said that what I'd seen of the King of Kings came as a great disappointment. So the king of Businiya is nothing more than that little old man in a khaki uniform no different from the uniforms of the soldiers around him, apart from a handful of medals? On his head was an enormous kepi that seemed far too big for him, and that made me laugh; but what troubled me most was his diminutive size. How can you be such a great king when you're so short? The king of Businiya had abruptly lost much of his prestige.

Mama finally gave in: yes, I might possibly have seen the king of Businiya. She must have made enquiries among the village 'intellectuals'. One day, in the sorghum field as always, she asked:

'So it's true, you weren't lying, you saw the king of Businiya?'

'Yes, I saw him, and right up close, too.'

'Tell me what he's like.'

I didn't dare describe the little man I'd seen. In the end, I told her:

'The king of Businiya looks like Papa.'

WOMEN'S AFFAIRS

When, with her hoe on her shoulder and her *pagne* hitched up to her knees, Stefania started for home from Gikombe – an old bog, almost gone dry, where she'd cleared a field so we could grow beans even in the dry season – I trotted after her, knowing we had a long walk ahead of us, not because of the distance, but because custom, politeness, respect, friendship, solidarity, and all of those at once required that we stop for a visit in every one of the huts lined up along the dirt road behind the row of coffee plants. Even if there was no sign of human presence, it would have been very rude to pass by a house without calling out a greeting: '*Yemwe abaha! Mwiriwe!* And you, the people of this place, hello!' But a simple hello was rarely enough for Stefania. She stopped at the little pathway that led through the coffee plants to the euphorbia hedge and repeated her salutation: '*Mwiriwe! Yemwe abaha!*'

That day, Mama might have stopped at Veronika's house. Veronika was in no hurry to answer. Rwandan etiquette dictates that nothing be done in haste. Even if Veronika had been eagerly waiting for Stefania's visit, it would have been unseemly to come running to meet her. First she began to make a little noise inside the hut, to show that she'd heard the visitor's call; then, after a suitable delay, she slowly walked out to the junction of the path and the dirt road, where Mama was waiting. They embraced at length, squeezing each other's backs and arms, murmuring words of welcome into each other's ears. Each wished the other a husband, many children, and many cows for as long as they lived. They asked after the families. They congratulated me on looking so healthy. Then, as slowly as ever, we all went off to sit down on a ragged mat in the back courtyard, beneath a banana tree.

The conversation took many long twists and turns – the children's health, the harvest, the rain's slowness in coming – and then little by little they worked their way around to the subject most on Veronika's mind: her two daughters, Formina and Illuminata. Formina, the first-born, was already almost an old maid. They couldn't find anyone to marry her. She was still wearing her *amasunzu*. That was one of Veronika's worries. The other, and no doubt the one that most tortured her, most shamed her, was Illuminata.

Because Veronika's younger daughter, very likely seeing her sister withering on the vine, hadn't waited for her mother and the village ladies to bring her a husband. She'd gone off to look for one in Karama, and she'd found him. Veronika reproached herself for giving her daughter a bad upbringing, even if at the same time she blamed all this – rightly, I think – on the deportation, on exile, on the persecutions that had overturned the rules of good behaviour the women of Nyamata were desperately struggling to maintain. Mama listened to the long litany of Veronika's griefs. She took great care not to interrupt: you must never interrupt when someone is speaking. All the while whisking a handful of fine grass over the already dry, cracked layer of mud on her feet and legs, she expressed her attentiveness with the occasional muted interjection – '*Heum! Heum!*' – a sign of approval and an encouragement to go on.

When Veronika reached the end of her lamentations, Mama began to speak Formina's praises, assuring her friend that they wouldn't fail to find her a husband in the end, telling her everything would work out, with the customs respected and the family's honour upheld.

And if we had nothing in the house for that evening's dinner, Stefania would casually mention that she couldn't think what she was going to cook for her children. There was no need to say anything more. To do so would have been indelicate, because Mama knew perfectly well that once she got to the end of the path, just before she started

125

down the road, Veronika would slip her a little basket of beans or sweet potatoes, just as she herself often did for the neighbours, saying, 'Take this, for the children.'

And Stefania would set off again, calling out greetings to Theodosia, Anasthasia, Speciosa, Margarita, Leoncia, paying a call on Pétronille, on Concessa . . .

Our last visit was always to Gaudenciana, our neighbour across the way. We found her in the *ikigo*, the back courtyard, her seven sons sitting idle around her. Mama pretended not to see them, because men, and even boys older than ten, don't belong in the *ikigo*; they can pass through it, but nothing more. Gaudenciana knew full well that Stefania didn't approve of the way she dealt with her children, and tried to justify herself: 'Ever since those young hoodlums from the Party set up their camp by the lake, we can't go and fetch water. They beat up the boys, they rape the girls. Imana, the God of the Rwandans, gave me seven sons. He left them in my care. When I die and Imana asks me, "What did you do with the seven boys I granted you?" I have to be able to tell him: "They're still there. Nobody killed them. I always made sure to watch over them." So it's my husband who fetches the water. I know, people make fun of him, it's no job for a man, but if they kill one of my boys, how can I answer Imana?' And Gaudenciana thought of moving, settling nearer the lake, not beside the road where the young men of the

Parmehutu Party had their camp, but in a place where no one would go looking for them, in the middle of the papyrus swamp, where clouds of mosquitoes attack you as soon as the sun goes down, where you're surrounded by crocodiles ... And once again Mama explained that her sons could indeed go to the lake, that the people had organised, they all went in groups, in a great convoy, taking advantage of the hours when the young men of the Party were busy somewhere else, and it was mostly the girls who had reason to be afraid ... Gaudenciana didn't answer, she looked at her sons. 'Anyway,' Mama would say, 'tomorrow I'll shave Butisi and Gastoni's heads. Send them over to me, surely they can cross the road.'

Our neighbours! What would we do without neighbours? There's always something you need to borrow from a neighbour. There's always a neighbour coming to borrow something from you. And if no one ever comes to borrow something, it makes you very sad. Don't people trust you? Do they suspect you're a poisoner? There's always some excuse for paying a call on the woman next door: maybe you need salt or water, some wood, a jug ... Someone might even ask you for one of your daughters, because the neighbour's husband isn't home tonight – he's gone off to Kigali – and she's alone with the little children and she'd feel more at ease with someone beside her, someone like Mukasonga, say, to keep her company. And the visit goes on and on, because politeness demands that the guest be walked home. It's very rude to let her go off all alone. But then, once you reach the neighbour's house, she'll obviously have to walk you back home, since you were kind enough to accompany her. These comings and goings can continue for some time. For as long as you have things to say to each other. And the most important things you've saved up, waiting to tell them in these obligatory back-and-forths. Those are secrets. You speak them in your quietest voice, you whisper them into your neighbour's ear.

Back before all this, back 'in Rwanda', as Stefania liked to say, you could walk from enclosure to enclosure through the banana groves. That way you could make many detours, pull some weeds on the way, or notice a prop collapsing under a heavy bunch of bananas, because a woman's hands must never be idle. But you had to be sure to leave time to say the things you had to say to each other. So you'd sit down halfway there. The woman carrying her baby would take the opportunity to nurse it or massage its plump little body. There was plenty of time to admire its dimples, especially the ones at the lower back. We call those 'the eyes of the bottom'.

Those 'eyes of the bottom' were important. Especially for girls. They were a mark of beauty, brought out by the belt of multicoloured beads young girls wore around their hips. So when the baby was still warm from its mother's body, she would use her index fingers to gently indent the 'eyes of the bottom', hoping the very delicate skin would keep the imprint of her motherly fingers.

Finally you reached the entrance to the neighbour's enclosure. You stopped under the towering bundles of bamboo framing the door. If the shadows told you it was time to go home and feed the children, you gave each other one final hug, reciting the customary good wishes once again.

But in Gitagata, no one dared see the neighbour back to her door. Out on the big road, we were always afraid we might meet up with the Party youth or the soldiers. We hurried along, there was no time to stop for a leisurely chat, no time for back-and-forths. And so we generally walked the visitor no further than the end of the path from the house to the road. We could have gone through the coffee plants, but we didn't dare trample the mat of fine grasses around those bushes the white people forced us to grow, and concerning which they forbade us all kinds of things. We didn't want any trouble with the agronomists from Karama, who kept our plantings under close surveillance. And so Stefania and her visitor stopped at the end of the path, beside the dirt road, and then turned back toward the house. When there was a great deal to say, they walked up and down that little path again and again. 'We're prisoners,' Mama sighed.

It was on Sunday afternoons, or even sometimes during the week, when they came home from the fields or a long day's work at one of their houses, often Stefania's or Marie-Thérèse's, that the women had their gatherings. They could roast corn, because while men refuse to eat in public, there's no such rule for women in unmixed company. They could also share a jug of sorghum beer – or, if the jug was empty, an infusion made by steeping the thick crust of sediment at the bottom of the jug. The first infusion produced a light beer, the second had no taste at all, the third filled your mouth with a horrible bitterness, and the women choked it down only so they wouldn't shame their hostess who had nothing to offer them but those pitiful dregs. 'After all,' my mother would sigh, 'you have to baptise the water somehow!'

But the real emblem of conviviality was the pipe. In Stefania's day, every woman in Rwanda smoked a pipe. It was a privilege that came with marriage. The bride was offered her first pipe at the party when she gave up her *amasunzu,* and everyone cheered as she took the first puff. Needless to say, women wouldn't smoke their pipes out in public, as men did: men smoked wherever they pleased, sitting by the door to their hut, gravely pacing the dirt road, at the market, after Sunday Mass. Women smoked only at home, in the *ikigo,* or sometimes in the fields, taking a break in the hottest hour of the day, behind the shelter of a bush. They complained of the men's habit of laying claim to the best tobacco, when it was the women who'd handled the delicate task of tending the plants and drying the leaves. The men left them nothing but crumbs. On Sundays, Mama would haggle relentlessly with my father for a few good leaves. She always got them in the end.

And so the women would fill their pipes, rolling a shred of leaf into a ball and piercing it with a basketry needle to provide the necessary aeration. They each took a puff, they swapped pipes, compared tobaccos, the pipes were passed from hand to hand. Is there any surer proof of friendship and trust than an exchange of pipes?

Many times I've asked my husband or children to give me a pipe as a present. They always laugh out loud. They think I'm joking. And yet I stand for many minutes at the window of the shop that sells pipes. I don't dare go in, that's a man's place. I soon come to my senses. How delicious could any tobacco be if there's no woman to trade pipes with?

The meetings in the *ikigo* were a genuine Parliament of women. Justice and external affairs were the men's concern. The elders, my father among them, ruled on civil complaints, resolved quarrels; when negotiation was possible, they led the difficult talks with the local governor, the mayor, the agronomists, the missionaries . . . With the soldiers and the Party youth, of course, there was nothing to discuss. Meanwhile, the women were in charge of education, health, economic matters, matrimonial tactics ... Everyone had a right to speak, for as long as she wanted; no one would interrupt. There was no majority and no minority. Decisions were made when everyone agreed.

Stefania, Marie-Thérèse, Gaudenciana, Theodosia, Anasthasia, Speciosa, Leoncia, Pétronille, Priscilla, and many more: those were the beneficent Mothers, the benevolent Mothers, the ones who fed, protected, counselled, and consoled, the guardians of the family and the community, the ones the killers slaughtered as if to wipe out the very sources of life.

The most urgent concern for mothers in Gitagata was their children's education. As soon as they could, first in Nyamata, and then in the villages where they'd been scattered, the exiles had opened schools. The teachers had had help from the missionaries, and they still depended on their support. Almost all the children in Gitagata went to school. The only ones who didn't were those who hadn't been baptised. You needed a Christian name to be allowed into school. That was the Fathers' rule. It must be said that the *abapagani* – the pagans – had a reputation as backward folk, who refused to join the inevitable march of progress. The missions, with their big churches, their red-brick buildings, their lights burning deep into the night with no need for a flame, were like pieces of the white people's countries that fell from the sky and landed right next door to us. Baptism was the only way in. There weren't many *abapagani* in Gitagata, but still, there were some: the Ngoboka family, for instance, who lived two houses away from us. Ngoboka was no die-hard pagan, no steadfast guardian of the traditions, no fierce foe of Christian teachings, no faithful follower of Ryangombe. He simply came from a very remote region of the Butare province, and had never crossed paths with the missionaries. Divine grace had overlooked him. At the same time, he seemed to mock our most venerable traditions. He had a grown-up son who used to go fishing in his little canoe on Lake Cyohoha. To the indignation of all Gitagata, the Ngoboka family ate fish, which, as everyone knows, can bring death to cows. Even if we had no cows any more, we found it deeply scandalous for a cowherd to ignore that interdiction: in one way or another, that could only bring sorrow upon us.

He also had three daughters, Mukantwari, Nyirabuhinja, and Nyiramajyambere, who stayed in the village, all alone, while the other children went off to class. On the way home from school, the most insolent children would shout, '*Abapagani! Abapagani!*' as they passed by the house of the little girls with no Christian names. On Sundays, they would sadly stare at the dressed-up crowd heading for the first, then the second, then the third Mass. Nonetheless, like everyone else, Ngoboka and his family observed

Sunday as a day of rest. We never saw them working in their field on the Lord's day.

Stefania pitied those poor children whose father's ignorance kept them isolated from the rest of us and the benefits of civilisation. With the agreement of the other women, it was decided that they would first see to Nyiramajyambere. Nyiramajyambere, 'the girl of progress', certainly had her destiny written in her name. Mama went and negotiated with Apollinaire Rukema, the catechist, to have her baptised. The girl was given a quick lesson in the Christian virtues. Stefania agreed to serve as her godmother, of course, and on her baptism Nyiramajyambere was given the lovely name of Gloriosa. All that was left to do was convince the schoolmaster, Bukuba, to allow a big girl of perhaps ten or even twelve into the younger children's class. Bukuba was hesitant. Many delegations of women finally put his qualms to rest, and Gloriosa started school. Stefania went on encouraging her, and she who didn't know how to read or write told her of all the many benefits of reading while my father opened his Bible and taught her to decipher a few words. Like most of Nyamata's schoolchildren, she didn't pass the national exam that allowed access to secondary school, but Marie-Thérèse's daughter Félicité welcomed her into her convent. She was taught sewing, 'civilised' cooking, and she learnt a few words of French, too. Her sisters followed the same path, and even found work in Kigali. Sometimes, in the course of their conversations, my mother would slip in a remark meant for my father: 'You see, I can convert pagans even without a rosary. Maybe Ryangombe had a hand in it, I don't know . . .'

If we talked about Suzanne in the *ikigo*, and sooner or later we always did, we had to take great care. Despite her deplorable reputation, we avoided any mention of her slovenly house, her wretched field, her children who wandered around in rags, covered with chigoe fleas. If we took all those precautions, it was because Suzanne filled a role in Gitagata that everyone found indispensable: she gave girls their prenuptial examination. For that reason, we were very happy to have Suzanne, and even if we scorned her under our breath, we never failed to greet her with the deepest respect, mingled with a touch of fear.

Talking about Suzanne meant, in one way or another, talking about sex. The subject of sex was absolutely forbidden. The words that refer to it were never spoken. We knew those words, of course, but we'd never heard them. How was it, I wonder, that everyone knew them? Was it the devil, Ryangombe in the flesh, as the Fathers would have said, who'd whispered those words in our ears? Nonetheless, girls' private parts were the subject of much preoccupation. There's no female circumcision in Rwanda, as there is in some other African countries. On the contrary, that precious nook where children come from was a thing to be carefully protected. From a girl's earliest childhood, it was kept covered, and most importantly its natural defences were reinforced. For a long time the little girl stuck close to her mother, like her shadow. But at around the age of ten, the mother told her daughter: 'Go see the woman next door, she has things to tell you, ask your older friends, they know what you have to do, ask Speciosa, at her age she ought to know.' And then she didn't say another word about it. It wasn't her place to initiate her daughter. Girls did that among themselves. They stretched apart the outer lips of the vulva, then folded them back like a tightly closed clam. I'm writing words that no Rwandan woman must ever write or speak. But after all, they're French words, so maybe they're not forbidden.

Before they got married, then, girls went to be examined by Suzanne, with deep apprehension. They'd heard the story of Margarita. The rumour was that she'd been shunned ever after. She'd come home in shame from her in-laws' house, across the Nyabarongo. Now she lived all alone, away from the others, in a little hut. No one ever saw her except when she was out in her field.

The girls went to Suzanne's after dark. They brought her presents. I don't know if that had any influence on the diagnosis; in any case, they generally went away relieved, their conformity with the demands of tradition confirmed.

Women didn't speak of such things in the *ikigo*, but when Suzanne's name was spoken, everyone knew what they were talking about.

The women also devoted much discussion to Fortunata's illness. Fortunata belonged to a very respected family of Gitagata. Her two older brothers, already married, had positions that brought them an unquestionable prestige: one was Rukema, the catechist I've already mentioned, and the other, Haguma, was a houseboy for one of the Belgian agronomists from Karama. Speciosa, the youngest daughter, had gone to Kigali to work for a white family. Since they'd been initiated into the labyrinthine mysteries of the missionaries' God or the strange ways of the Europeans, we unhesitatingly placed them in the exalted category of the evolved people. As for Fortunata, she'd stayed behind in Gitagata to look after Cecilia, her aged mother, very frail, almost an invalid. She was a brave and tireless girl, and everyone admired her. We called their house not 'Cecilia's house' but 'Fortunata's house'. Mothers with bachelor sons built up all manner of glorious plans around her: happy would be the woman who had Fortunata as a daughter-in-law!

And then one day Fortunata disappeared. Suddenly we stopped seeing her in the field or on the path to the lake, or even after Sunday Mass. The girls said she'd stopped joining the others to touch up her *amasunzu*. Everyone was worried: we realised she'd stopped leaving her house, we heard she wouldn't get up from her mat, that she trembled all over, that she groaned night and day but never said where she was hurting, only repeated over and over the name Théoneste, a name that meant nothing to anyone in Gitagata. In the women's opinion, it was a very strange illness, of a kind never before seen in Gitagata, or even in Rwanda, as far back as even the oldest of them could remember. And neither could they understand why her aged mama didn't come for advice from her neighbours: if everyone put their heads together, the women would surely have ended up finding the proper plant or charm to cure Fortunata.

I don't know who revealed the name of the mystery illness, or how the news spread through the village and beyond. Fortunata was suffering from lovesickness. Lovesickness! We'd never heard of any such thing! How did Fortunata ever come down with that? Love had to be one of those sicknesses white people get. But what could we do against a white people's disease? Some accused Speciosa of bringing it home from Kigali, and when she came back to Gitagata she was immediately quarantined. They had to make perfectly sure the lovesickness wouldn't spread. As we understood it, teenage girls were the most vulnerable. Mothers kept them under strict surveillance, wouldn't let them go out. Children, especially little girls, were forbidden to walk past Fortunata's house. A new path to the school was cleared so they could avoid the cursed place, by way of a long detour. Lovesickness was all anyone talked about. Even the men had their opinions, and children composed songs that – at a safe distance from

Fortunata's house – they sang at the top of their lungs: '*Indwara y'urukundo! Indwara y'urukundo!* It's the lovesickness! It's the lovesickness!'

Fortunata's brothers were of course gravely troubled by the scandal their sister's illness was causing. They launched their own investigation to unmask the poisoner, the one whose evil spell had taken hold of poor Fortunata. After a long and elaborate inquest, they concluded that the cruel spell-caster was a certain Théoneste who lived far from Gitagata, beyond Nyamata, on the banks of the Nyabarongo. The brothers went to see him and vigorously explained that, since he was the one who'd infected their unfortunate sister with the terrible lovesickness, he would have to accept the consequences, which is to say bring Fortunata into his home, be responsible for her in her present state, the state his loathsome drugs had put her in. Whether willingly or by force, Théoneste accepted the two brothers' proposal. And so they sent Fortunata off to him at once, and from what we were later told, she soon regained her good health.

All of Gitagata breathed a deep sigh of relief when Fortunata went on her way. The dread lovesickness had been eradicated. Girls could once again dream of their future marriages, and mothers could work to seek out the men they thought the best catch for their daughters.

'I saw poor Claudia go by again,' Stefania would say. 'Still wearing *amasunzu* at her age! We have to do something for her.' The women of the *ikigo* didn't hesitate to lay the most underhanded traps to find a husband for girls who couldn't manage on their own. That was how it was with Claudia.

Claudia had lost her mother. She was an only child, and so she had to look after her aged father, who could no longer work in the field or keep up the enclosure. But Claudia was a brave young woman, and above all she was exceptionally strong. When she went to fetch water, she carried jugs on her head that no man could have lifted. Everyone admired her massive thighs, her hairy legs, her majestic walk, favourably compared with an elephant's. Her wide hips gave ample promise of abundant fertility. Even if her physique didn't perfectly live up to the canons of Rwandan beauty, no one could understand why boys always found some reason to refuse a girl so manifestly built to till the soil and bring many children into the world. Nonetheless, we had our suspicions: Claudia's mother had died after a long illness that kept her closed up in her house. Such an illness, which they'd clearly tried to hide from the village, could only have been caused by the evil machinations of a poisoner. There was every reason to fear that the curse would extend to the entire family, not sparing Claudia or even Claudia's children. No one wanted to deal with that.

And so Claudia stayed unmarried. She could have gone to Kigali, as others had. They always came back from Kigali with a husband. But Claudia was as strait-laced a girl as could be, and her father Francisco rigorously enforced a respect for tradition. He was known in the village as a man who jealously guarded his honour, and they said he'd sworn to his wife that he'd keep a close watch over their only daughter's.

The years went by, and Claudia still didn't have a husband. The women of Gitagata decided it was high time they found her one. They set their eyes on Karangwa. He was an ageing bachelor, but still a fine catch, because he worked in Karama, as a houseboy or a gardener, I can't recall which. Exceptionally for an unmarried man, he didn't live with his parents: he lived alone, in his own house. That was very likely why the women had chosen him.

Karangwa worked all week long in Karama. Like my brother Antoine, he only came back to Gitagata on Saturday, and then left on Sunday. That gave the women a chance to devise and implement their scheme. Claudia approved of the ruse, and evidently took part without the slightest hesitation. One Saturday, then, Claudia was brought into Karangwa's house before he got home. She hid in the darkest corner: there was little risk of Karangwa's discovering her when he came home after draining several jugs of beer with the other bachelors. All night long, then,

Claudia huddled in the corner, not moving, scarcely breathing, and then, at the first light of dawn, a neighbour woman comes and knocks at Karangwa's door, and of course she immediately spies Claudia, who has burst out of her dark corner and shown herself very clearly next to Karangwa's bed. Just as planned, the neighbour begins to shout, as loudly as she can, '*Yemwe! Mamawe!* Karangwa has abducted Claudia! Karangwa has abducted Claudia!' And on hearing her cries, everyone hurries out of their houses. Soon an enormous crowd gathers around Karangwa's house, shouting, 'Karangwa abducted Claudia! He abducted Claudia!' The women let out a piercing *Yiiiiii! Yiiiiii!* Francisco comes running. He calls on Karangwa to marry his daughter. She's been found in his house, she spent the night there. The entire village is witness: he abducted Claudia. Karangwa struggles to stammer out some sort of answer. But it's too late, people are already bringing jugs of beer, the women of the conspiracy are already intoning songs in praise of the bride-to-be, the girls have already begun to dance. Claudia's father and Karangwa's family have taken things in hand. The traditions will be respected, and Claudia will be given a husband. There's nothing left to do but celebrate!

Pregnancy was of course a major preoccupation for women. To have a child was to acquire at last the consideration, respect, and power all women aspired to. A young bride was expected to become pregnant as soon as possible. If his wife was slow to announce that she was with child, worry would gnaw at the husband, he would feel the weight of the other men's disdainful stares, and the village gossips' tongues would wag freely. Soon people would be discreetly advising him to renounce his wife, who was obviously sterile. Which is why, in Rwanda, pregnancies could sometimes wander and drift, they didn't always stay in place, they travelled through all the various parts of the mother-to-be's body. The young woman would announce to her husband: 'I'm pregnant, but the baby's gone into my back.' That curious phenomenon might have been caused by an evil spell cast by a poisoner, who knows, maybe a jealous neighbour, or it could be a curse from further away, but in any case it came as no surprise to anyone, the baby wandered all over its mother's body, her back, her neck, her knee . . . No one found that particularly troubling: the baby would surely go back where it belonged in the end.

The baby's peregrinations could last for months, as long as two years, but for Nakereti's wife Madame – whose strange name (and it really was a name, not a nickname) and oddly pale skin caused lots of talk: 'Yet another,' Stefania would sigh, 'whose mother's confession went on all night long' – the women counted: 'This is the fifth sorghum harvest since Madame became pregnant, and still no sign of the baby!' The villagers came to feel that Madame and her endless pregnancy were putting them in danger. A five-year pregnancy, it simply couldn't be! Some very powerful spell must have been placed on Madame. They had to keep their distance from her, had to avoid coming near her at all costs, walk the other way should they meet up with her. The unhappy couple found themselves outcasts, because all the men jeered at Nakereti, who believed everything his wife told him, and was still naively waiting for the baby to move back to the belly it never should have left. Some suspected that he too had been stricken by the dread lovesickness. Stefania and a few others had a different opinion. Madame and Nakereti's house, they observed, shared a wall with Tito's, Tito being the shopkeeper who was among those arrested by the soldiers in 1963. They'd also taken his little boy Apollinaire. They threw him into the truck with his father. Madame had seen all that, heard all that. According to Stefania, the baby had felt the terror tormenting its mother. That baby was in no hurry to come into the world. A world where children were murdered.

We never found out if Madame finally gave birth to the itinerant baby, because after the massacres of 1967, when so many young men were killed, they managed to flee to Burundi. We never heard from them again . . .

The rapes. No one wanted to talk about them. No one could talk about them. We had nothing in our traditions to help us deal with that family-shattering catastrophe.

Before, 'in Rwanda', if an unwed girl became pregnant, she went into hiding, she disappeared, people said she'd gone to Kigali, or even further away, to Burundi, to Usumbura as we said in those days. In any case, she was not to bear her child in the family house. It wasn't so much moral condemnation that banished the poor girl as the fear that any breach of the rules of an orderly society might bring down on the family, and then the entire community, a succession of disasters striking everything from the fertility of the fields to the fecundity of the women and cows. The young woman and her baby generally came back to their families in the end, but wariness and apprehension still surrounded a child born outside the norms all Rwandans respected.

But what does tradition have to say when your daughters are prey for the young men of the Party, who have been inculcated with the idea that raping a young Tutsi woman is a revolutionary act, an irrevocable right for the people of the majority? Who will bear the crushing weight of the sorrow you struggle in vain to conceal? The girl-mother, now a living curse, shunned by all and sinking into loneliness and despair? The family, plagued by remorse for not having been able to protect one of their own, now finding themselves prudently kept to one side by the entire village? And the child, the child of hate, what sorrows will he bring you?

It was the rape of Viviane that made all the women question the treatment imposed by tradition. Viviane was a very young woman, still a teenager. The mothers held her up as a model of good behaviour to their daughters when they showed a wild streak. She committed the imprudence of going to fetch water at Lake Cyohoha alone, at an hour when the young men of the Party were in their camp, whiling away their leisure time over a few cases of beer, boasting of their brutal attacks on the Tutsis, planning more. Not seeing her daughter come back, Viviane's mother warned the other women, who went to tell the men. They immediately set off down the dirt road to Cyohoha. Well before they reached the lake, they saw Viviane's calabash by the road, broken. A little further on, in a thicket, they found Viviane herself, bloodied and covered with bruises. She'd clearly been raped. They went off to get a stretcher made of strips of bamboo, used to transport the gravely ill or the dead. Two men carried the stretcher on their shoulders. They crossed through the village. Everyone could see Viviane and the blood stains on her *pagne*. There was nothing to hide.

Despair fell over the village. We implored the aid of the Virgin Mary and Ryangombe both. Needless to say, we wept for Viviane, but we were also weeping over the many new miseries that surely lay in wait for the people of Gitagata because the rape had been made visible to all.

But this time solidarity and pity were stronger than tradition. The customary exclusion was not inflicted on Viviane and her family. Stefania and a few other women came to treat her. The wounds healed, but soon it was discovered that Viviane was pregnant. Still the village women went on offering her all their aid and counsel. She gave birth in the family house. The matrons, the women people always called on to be with mothers in labour, helped Viviane bring her baby into the world, a beautiful baby, a boy.

All the same, the women were convinced that they had to ward off the curse Viviane and her child were surely bearing. They gathered in the back courtyard to talk it over. Huddled behind the termite mound, I did my very best to go unnoticed so I could listen in on the deliberations. Mama repeated one of her favourite adages: 'Water purifies everything'. And little by little the entire assembly arrived at an agreement that a ritual cleansing was the answer: with great care, they would wash every inch of Viviane's and her child's bodies. But what water might have a purifying force strong enough to drive out the evil infused in the mother and her baby by the rape? The fetid water of Lake Cyohoha obviously wouldn't do. Rainwater seemed unlikely to work. They'd need to draw the cleansing water from the Rwakibirizi spring. That was the one spring in the Bugesera, and it never ran dry. The water gushed out as if from the very entrails of the earth. It had sprung up in the time of Rwanda's birth. Coming home from his exile, Ruganzu Ndori, one of the founding kings of Rwanda, had made a stop at Rwakibirizi, and the water spurted out as soon as he thrust his spear into the ground. The king brought fertility and abundance with him: the water of Rwakibirizi, born of his sovereign authority, had the power to vanquish any curse.

They chose two very young virgin girls to fetch the water, girls whose purity couldn't be questioned. To carry the water, they gave them two big churns (and it wasn't easy finding churns among our people, we who had lost all our cows!). The women accompanied them: all the way to the spring, they sang the praises of Ruganzu Ndori, prudently falling silent when they saw someone coming.

The women organised the ritual down to the smallest detail. It had to take place in the bush, the home of the Spirits. But the Spirits are most likely to show themselves where two paths meet, so they chose a crossroads far from prying eyes and lined the ground with fine grasses.

On the appointed day, the women, Viviane, and her child set off well before sunup, in the dark of night. They had to perform the rite at the auspicious hour, which is to say before the sun comes up but when the sky is already growing pale with its new light. I didn't see the ceremony: I wasn't allowed to follow my mother. I was too young, and no doubt too talkative. It's not good to reveal the secrets that open the world of the Spirits. In any case, the officiants didn't bring the churns back to the village: they hurried to bury them deep in the mud of the swamp.

The Rwakibirizi water did indeed lift the curse that Viviane's rape had brought on the village: no one could doubt it. It was even conceivable to throw a party to welcome the child whose father's name no one wanted to know. This wasn't an *Ubunyano*, Viviane's son was already too old for that, but they gave him a name, Umutoni – 'He-is-with-us' – and all the children of Gitagata saw him as their brother from that moment on. Viviane's honour was restored, though her status nonetheless remained faintly uncertain. She wasn't a girl any more, she couldn't wear *amasunzu*, but neither was she a wife. Nor was she a married woman. And so she was considered a widow, and only a widower could marry her.

In 1994, rape was one of the weapons of the genocide's perpetrators. Many of them carried AIDS. And all the water of Rwakibirizi, and all the water of all the springs in Rwanda, would never be enough to 'cleanse' the victims of the shame of the perversions inflicted on them, or the stigma – for they were thought to be carriers of death – that made them pariahs in the eyes of so many. But in themselves, in themselves and their rape-begotten children, they found the living source of courage, the force to survive, to defy their assassins' plans for them. Mother Courage is everywhere in the Rwanda of today.

Do the spirits of the dead speak to us through our dreams? I'd so like to think they do. In a notebook, I write down this nightmare that has obsessed me in my sleep for some time.

The classroom door bursts open and out pours a torrent of schoolchildren, little girls in blue dresses, boys in shorts and khaki short-sleeved shirts. They make a long, silent column, but they don't scatter, as they usually do, once they've come through the little eucalyptus wood that separates the schoolyard from the dusty grounds of the marketplace. They all start down the path that leads to the Gako camp, on the Burundi border. 'Where are you going, children?' I want to ask. 'Why aren't you heading home?' But I also know that I know the answer, because I'm one of the little girls, me, Mukasonga, I'm walking next to my friend Candida, and in front of me and behind me there's Immaculée, Madeleine, Speciosa, and also Alphonsine and Viviane . . .

I know we're going off to pick flowers. The Father asked us to do that at the end of Mass: 'Next Sunday is the Feast of Corpus Christi, so we'll need flowers for the altar, and many more for the procession.' And after his lesson the catechist Kenderesire told us again: 'You have to go and pick flowers, white flowers for the altar of the Good Lord, and many, many petals for the Marian Procession.' And before we left the classroom the schoolteacher Désiré told us yet again: 'Now, don't forget, you've got to go pick flowers for the altar of Our Lord, and for the shower of petals you'll throw in the air before the golden rays of the monstrance.'

Now the children are at the foot of a high hill. It's completely white, covered with white flowers. The children run, run up the hillside. I can't follow them. I'm not a little girl any more. I shout: 'Don't go up that hill, there's nothing but sharp stones: that's Rebero, that's where the people were killed.' The white flowers sway back and forth as the children run by. They make a grating sound, a grinding sound, a clicking or crackling like dry wood. I plug up my ears. I shout, 'Come back, children, come back . . .'

In the church, the children are carrying bouquets, sprays, armloads, bundles of white sticks. I tell the children:

'Those aren't flowers you've picked . . .'

'No,' Candida answers. 'Look closely. See what we're laying on the altar of Jesus, before the statue of Mary.'

At the foot of the altar of Jesus, at the foot of the statue of Mary, I see piles of bones: the skeletons of the men, women, and children of Nyamata lie strewn over the floor of the church.

'Do you recognise them?' Candida asks me. 'Look closely, they're here, and I'm with them, and your family, and Stefania, do you recognise them?'

Now Candida is only a shadow, growing ever dimmer, and her voice is only a distant echo:

'Do you have a *pagne* big enough to cover them all, every one of them . . . every one . . . every one?'